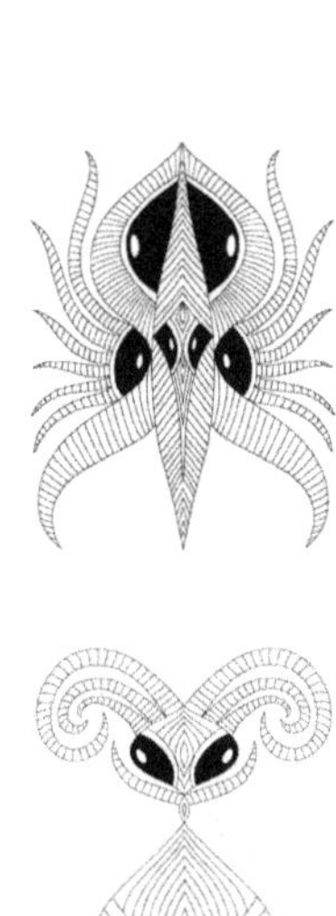
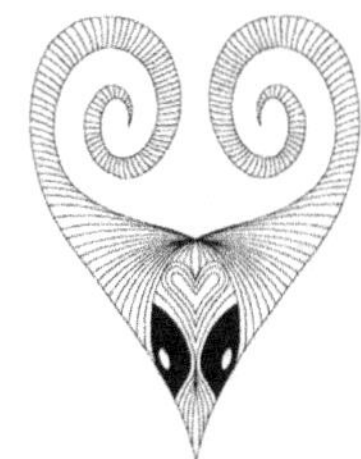
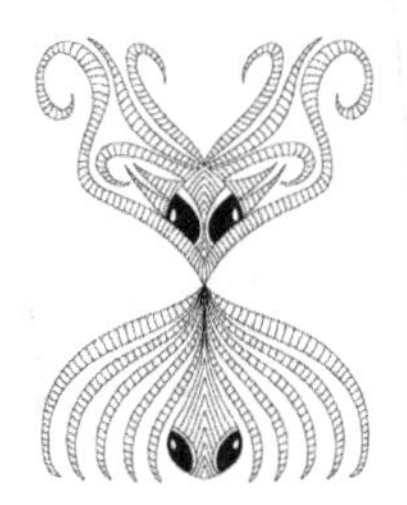

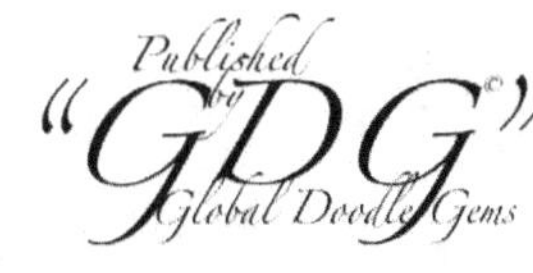

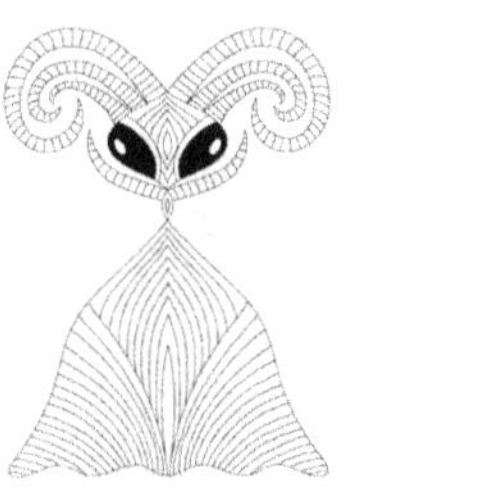
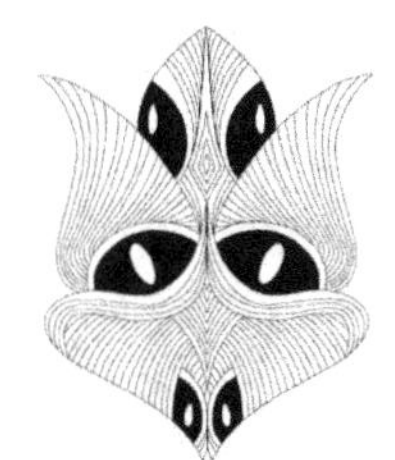
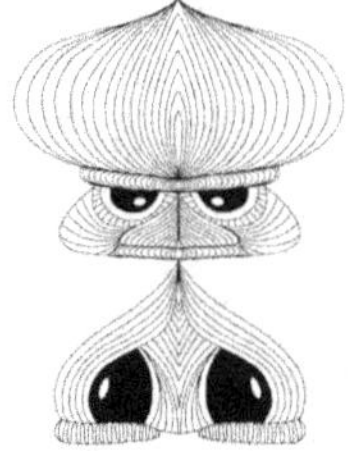
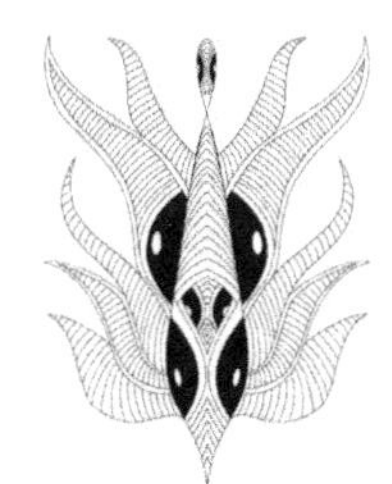

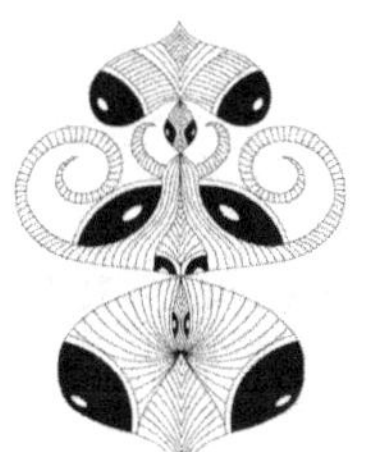
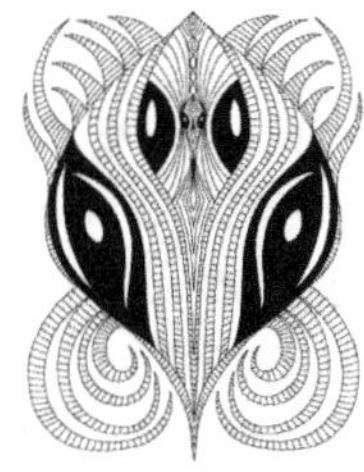
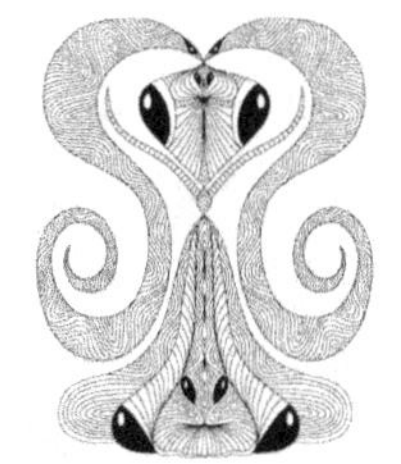
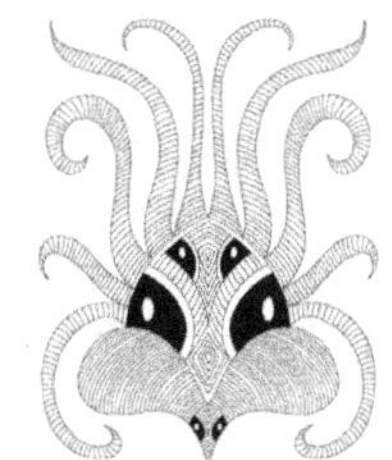

These Weirdie's
belong to the collection
of

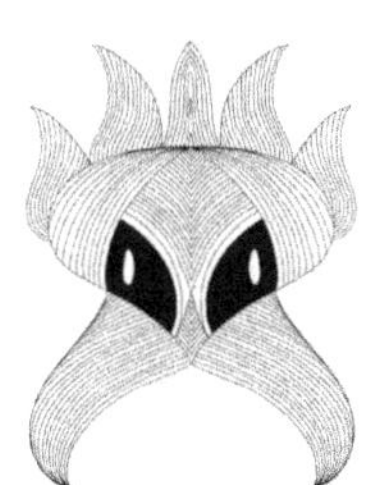
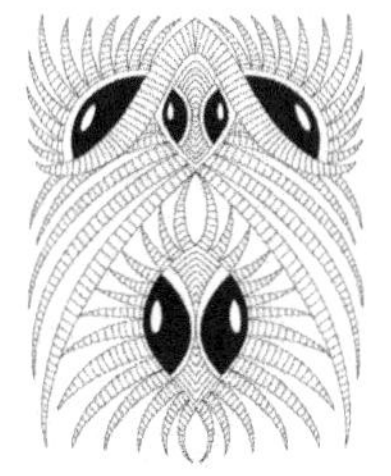

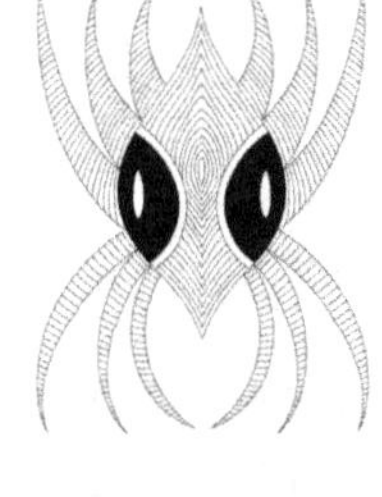
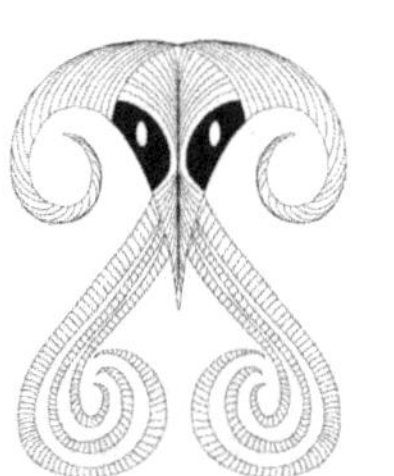
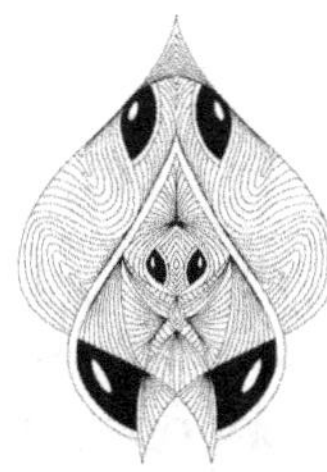

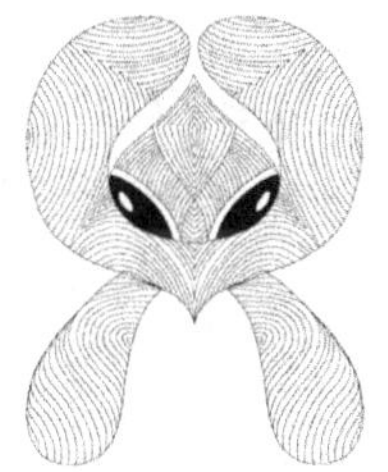
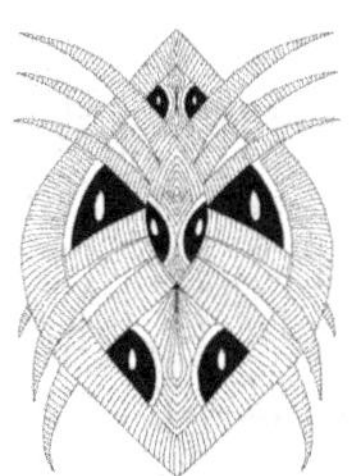
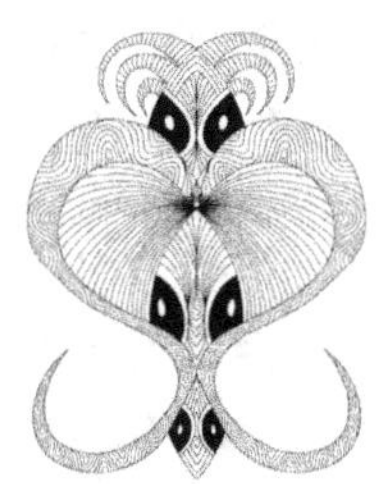

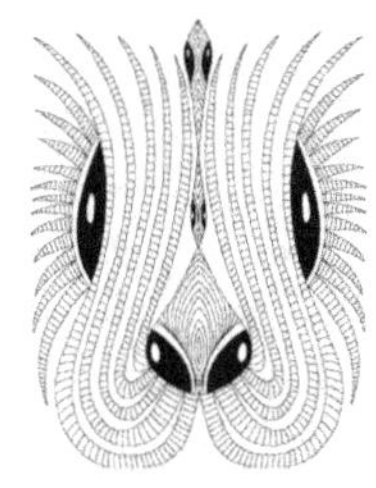
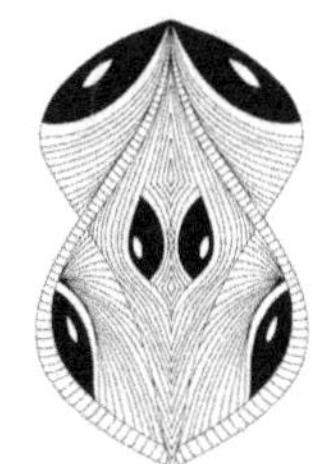
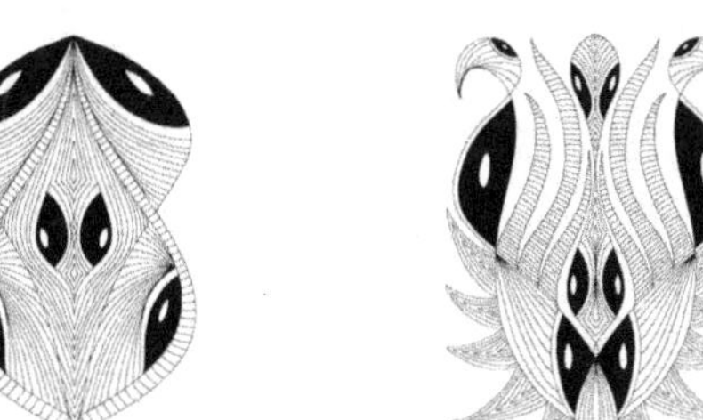
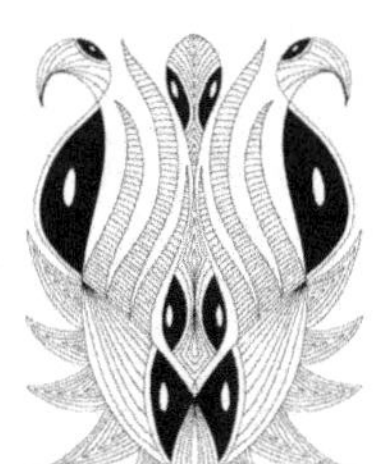

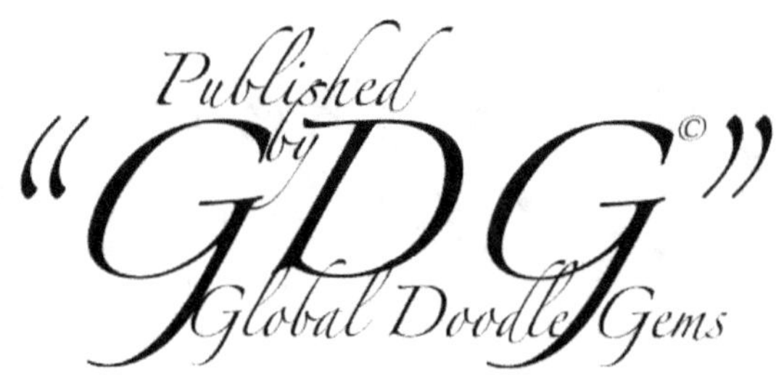

Share your colored versions with us ! We love seeing your results
and hearing from you
we are social !

The Official FB book page, stay on top of what we have in the works !
www.facebook.com/AMVWART
The Community group, share your colored pages, meet the artists, enjoy exclusive freebies, take part in community Charity books and so much more......
www.facebook.com/groups/ColorAWeirdieADay
Follow us on Twitter.... @GlobalDoodlegem
We are on Instagram too
@globaldoodlegems for instagram
...and if you are not social like that we have a blog
globaldoodlegems.wordpress.com

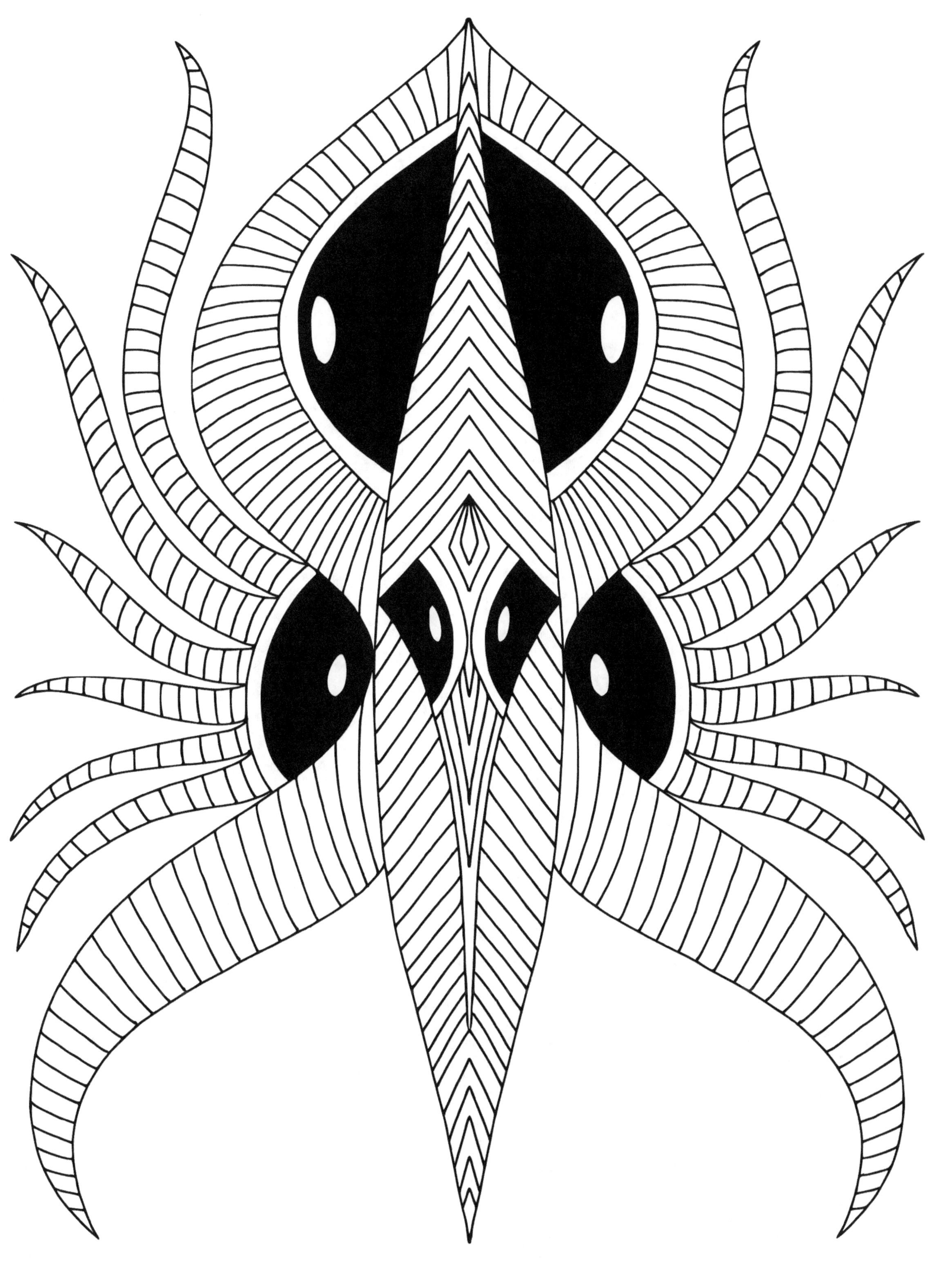

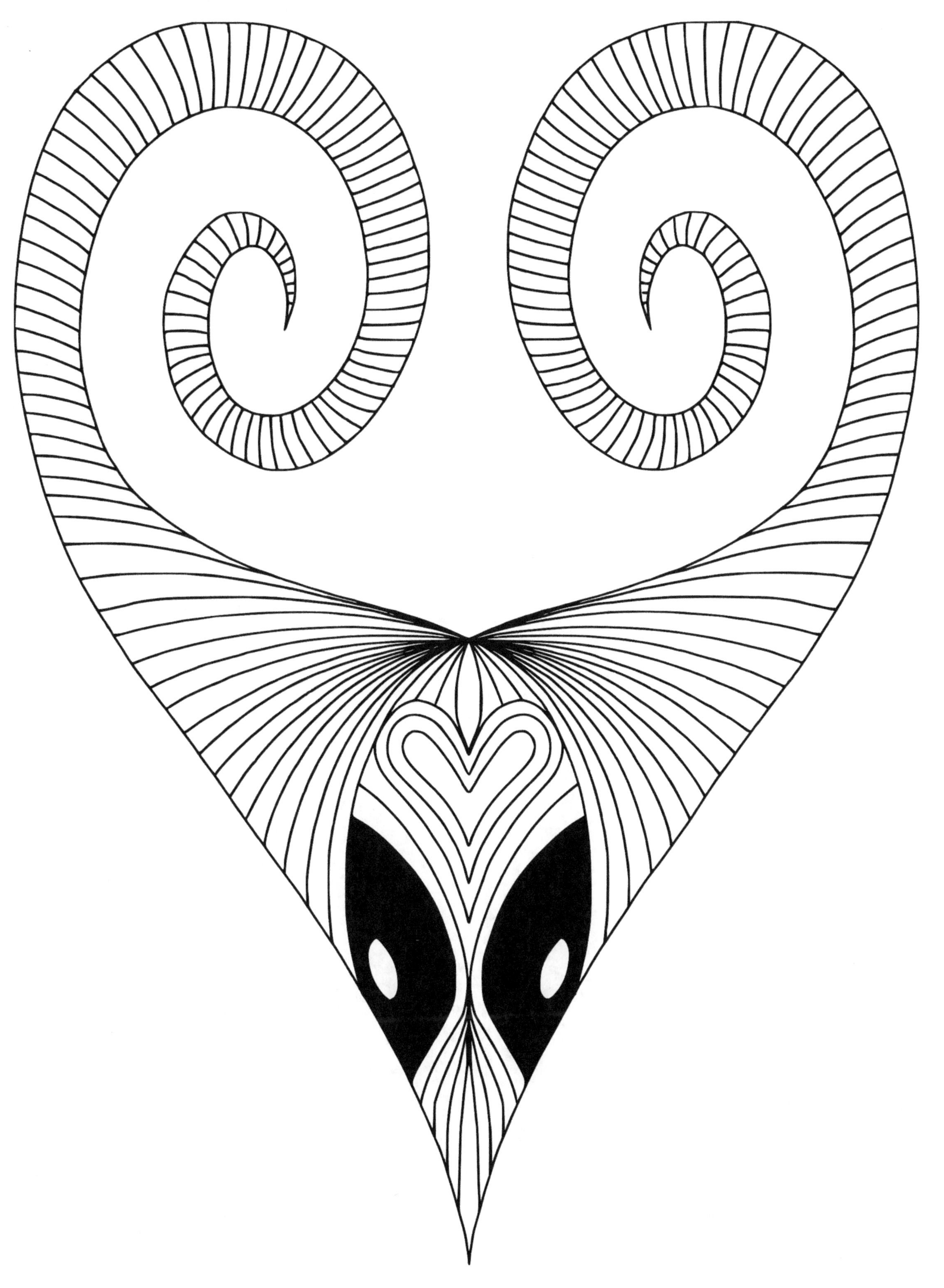

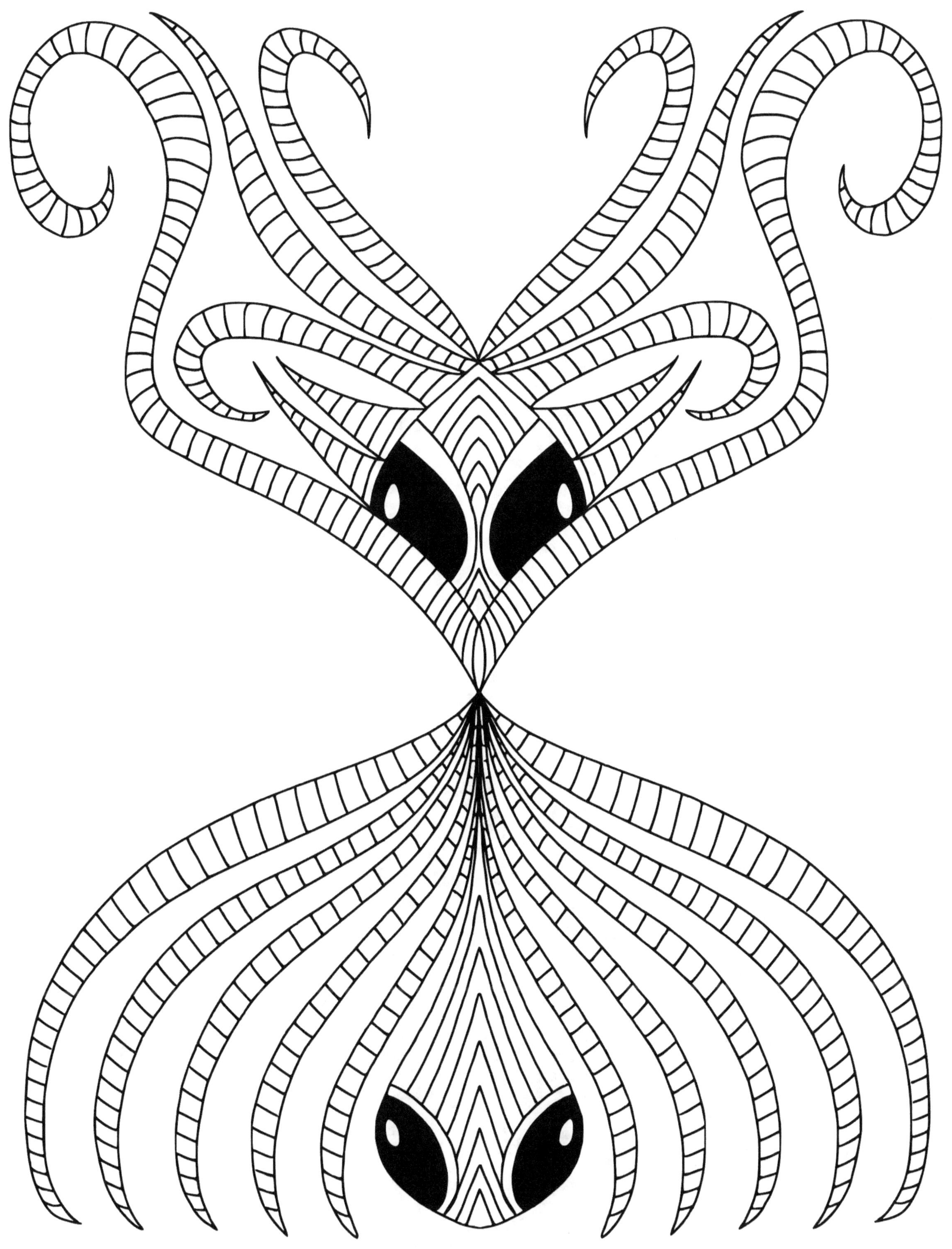

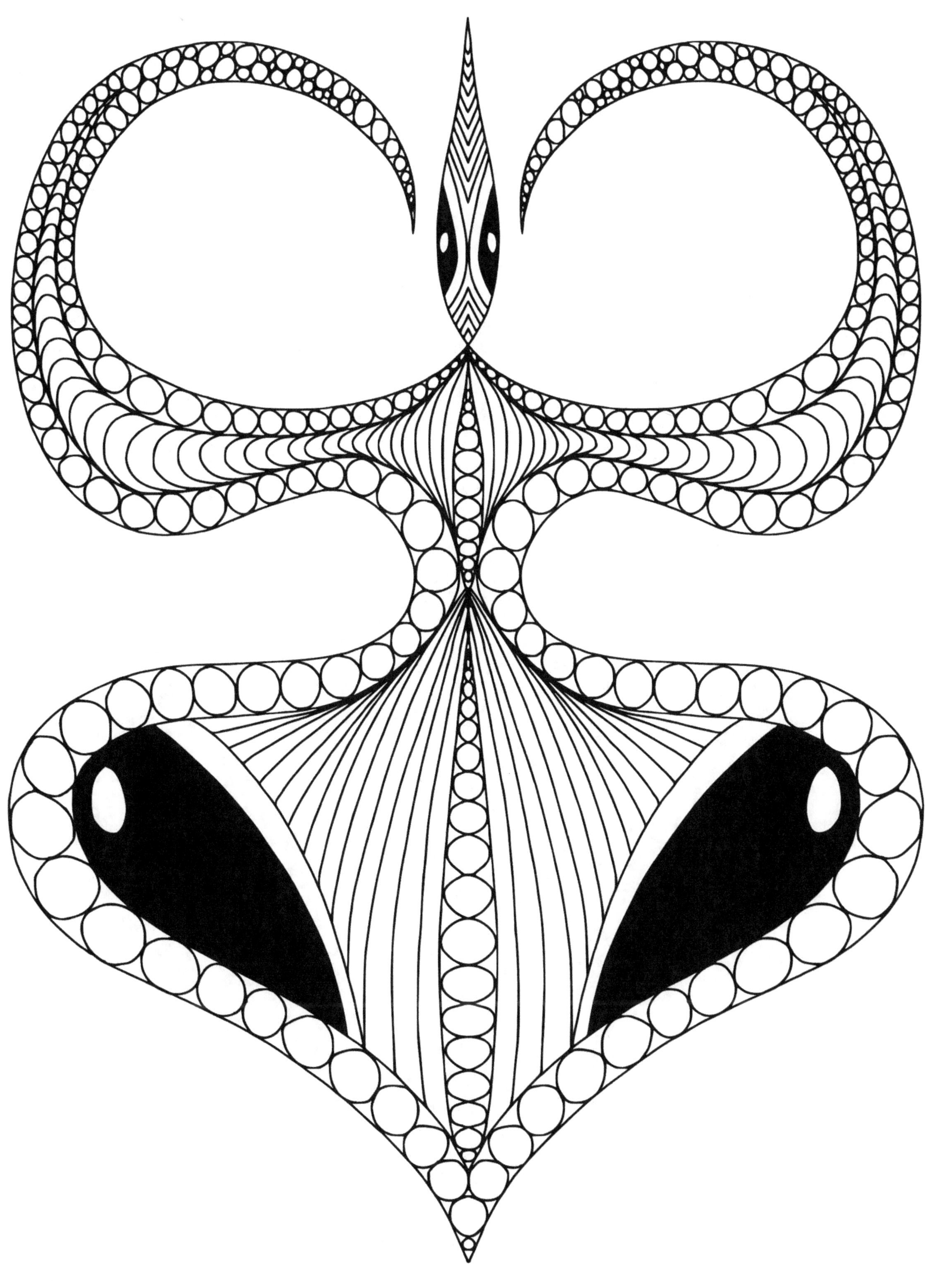

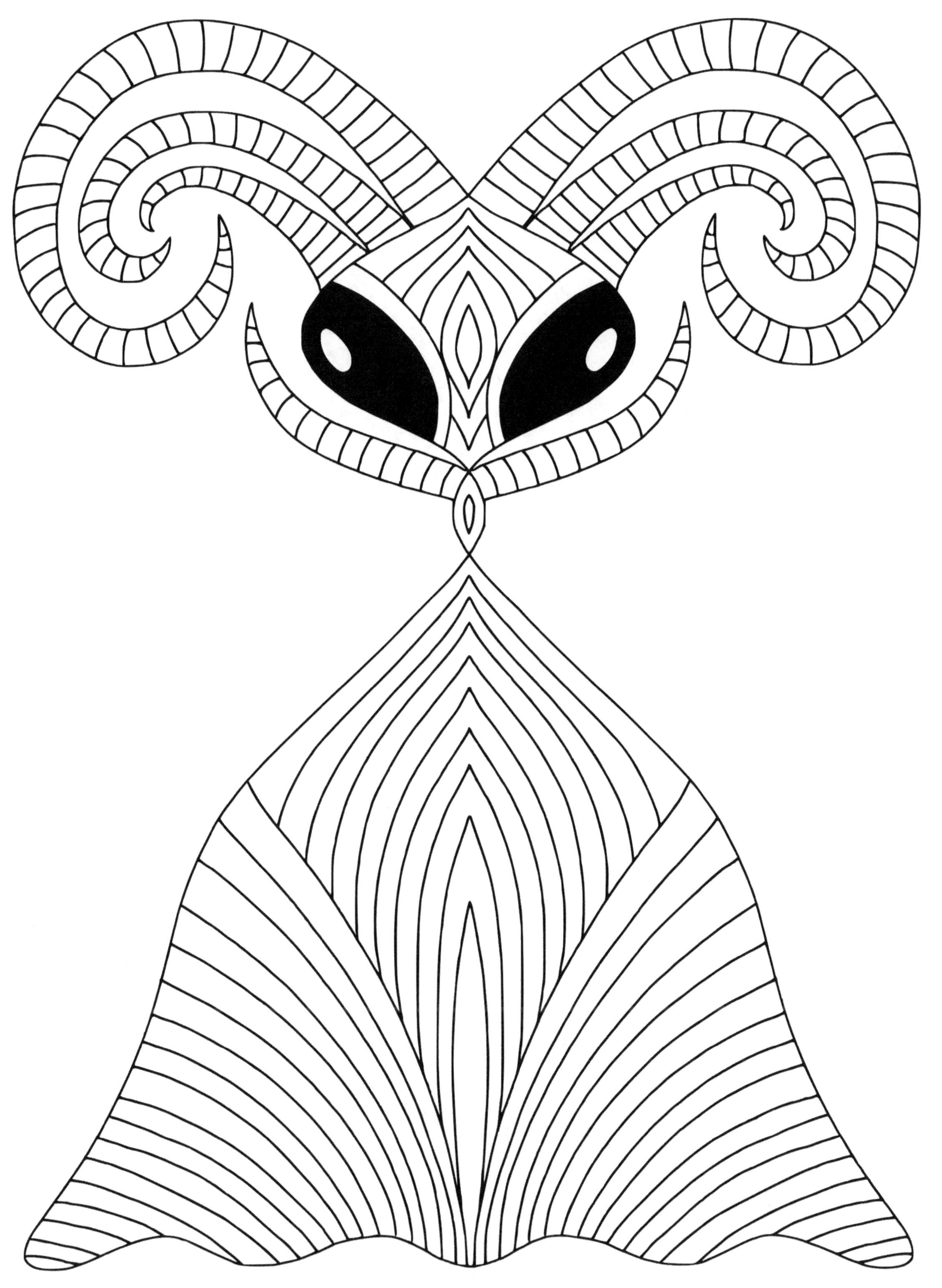

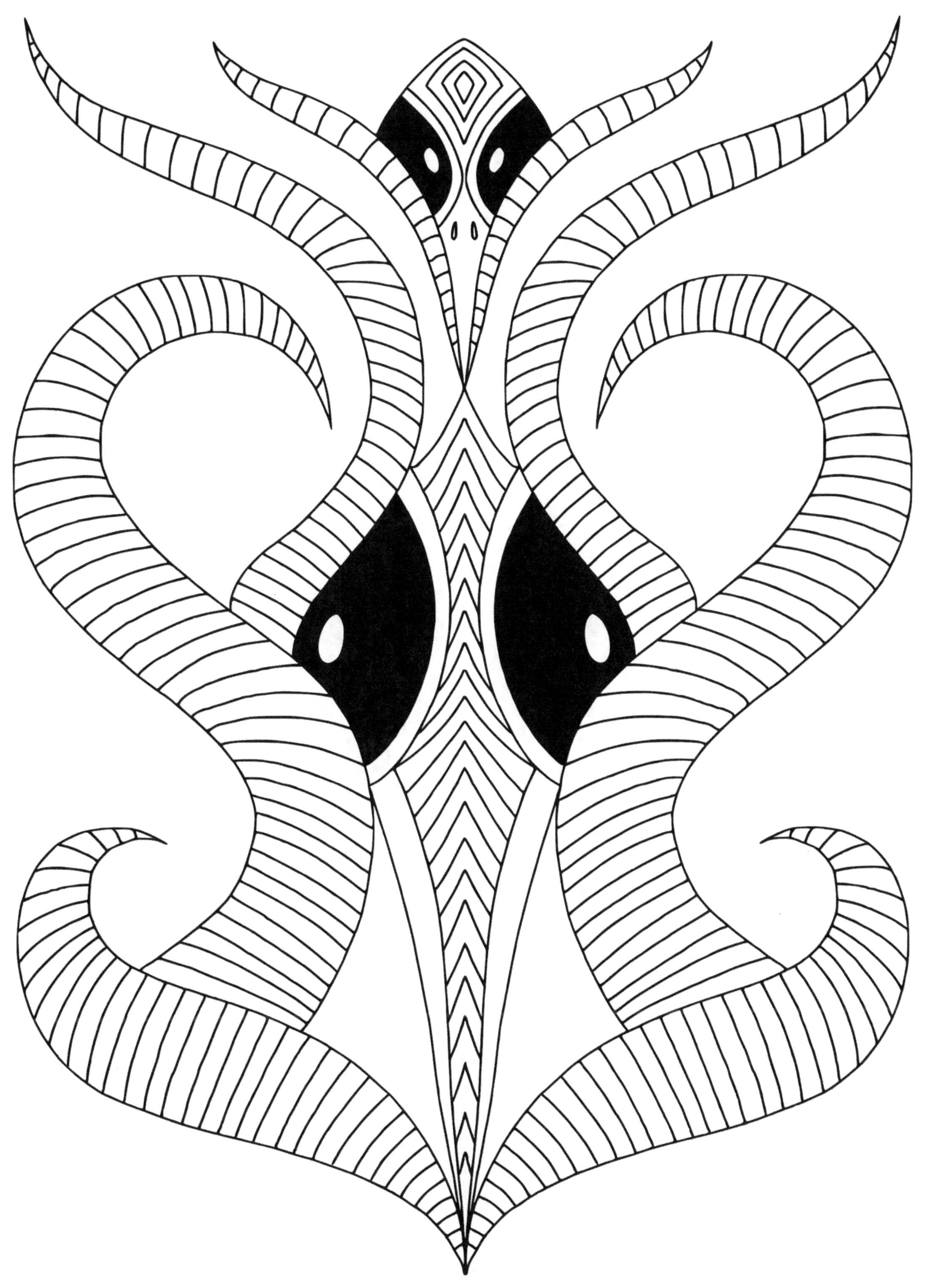

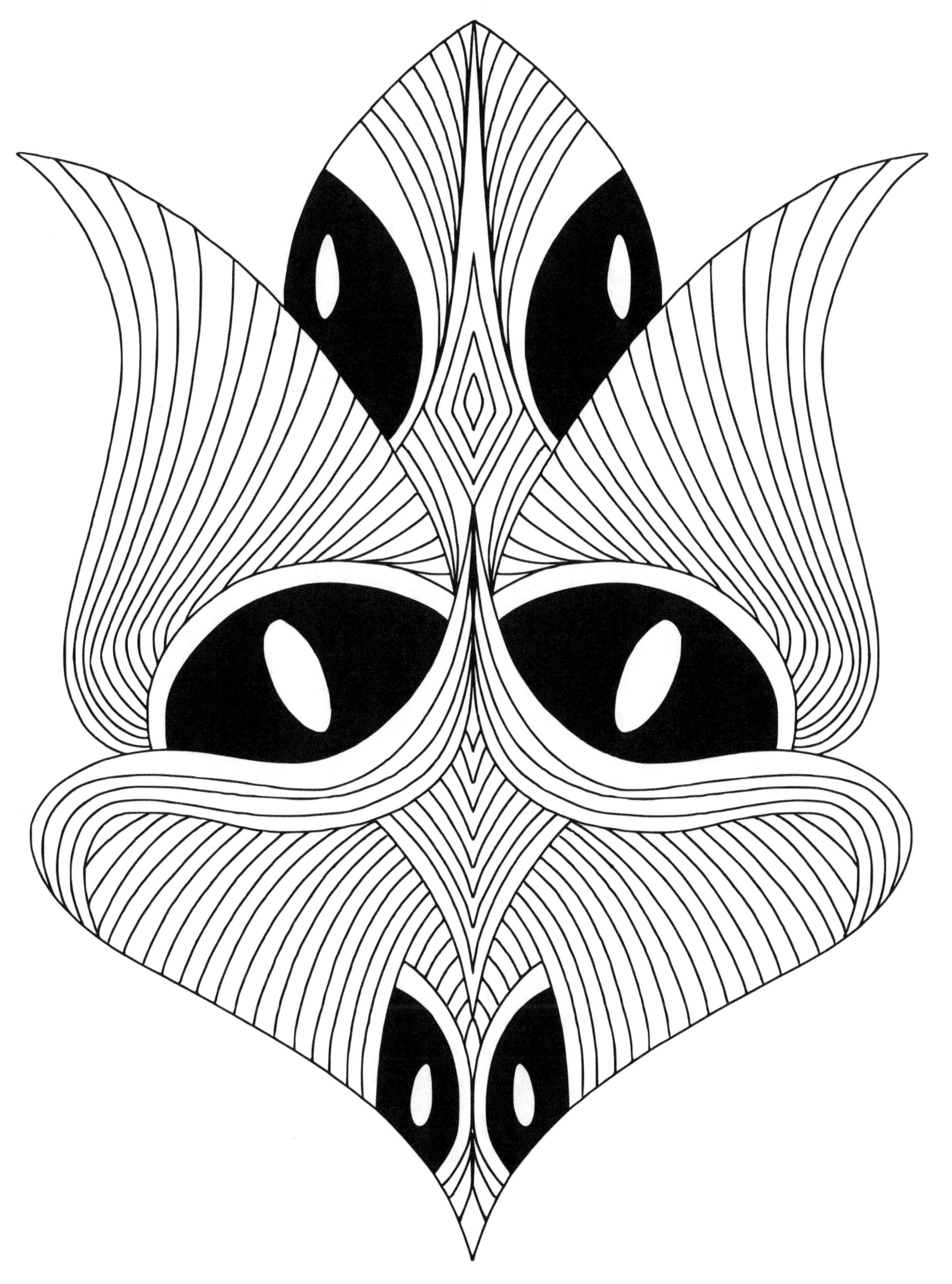

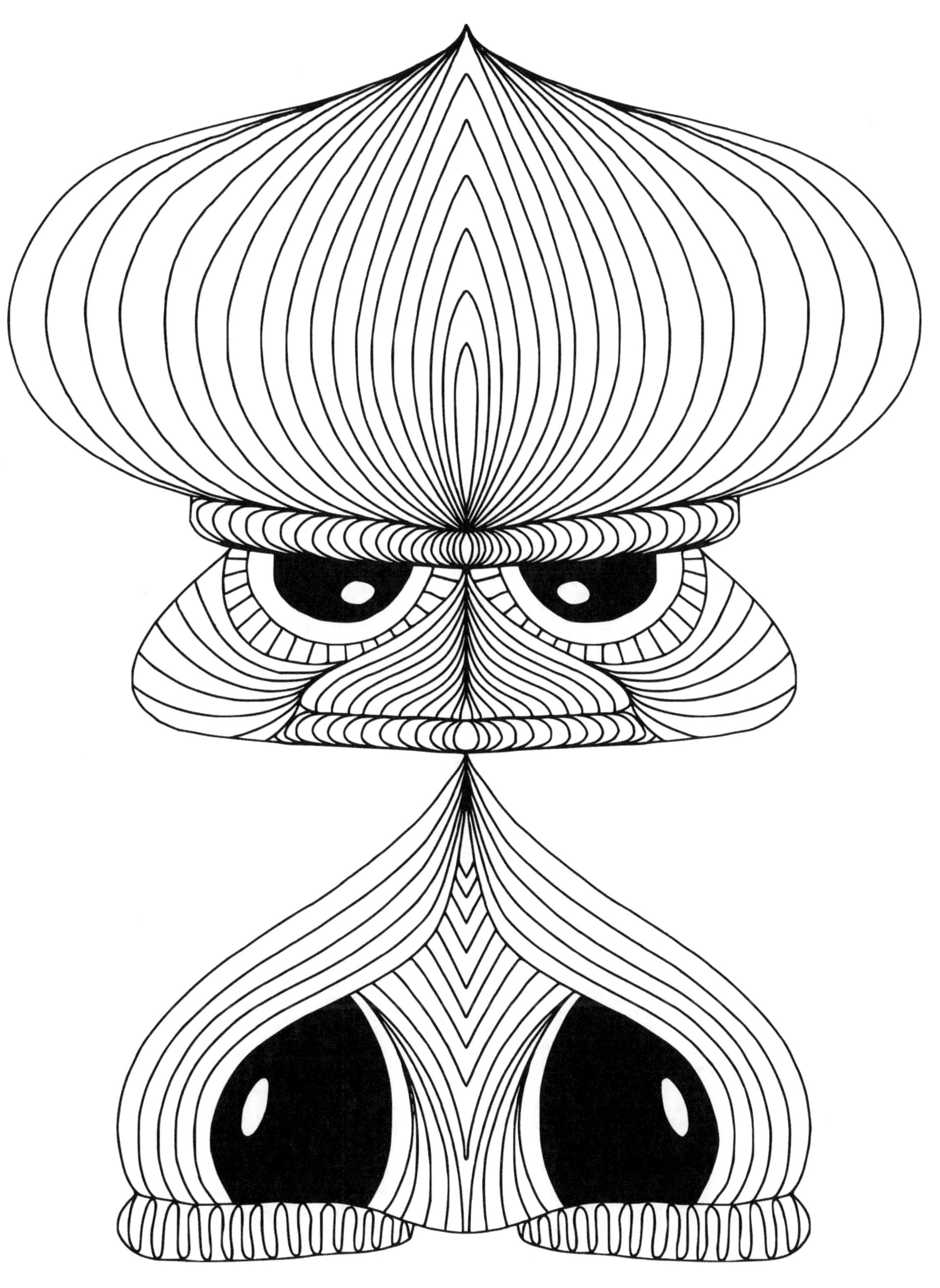

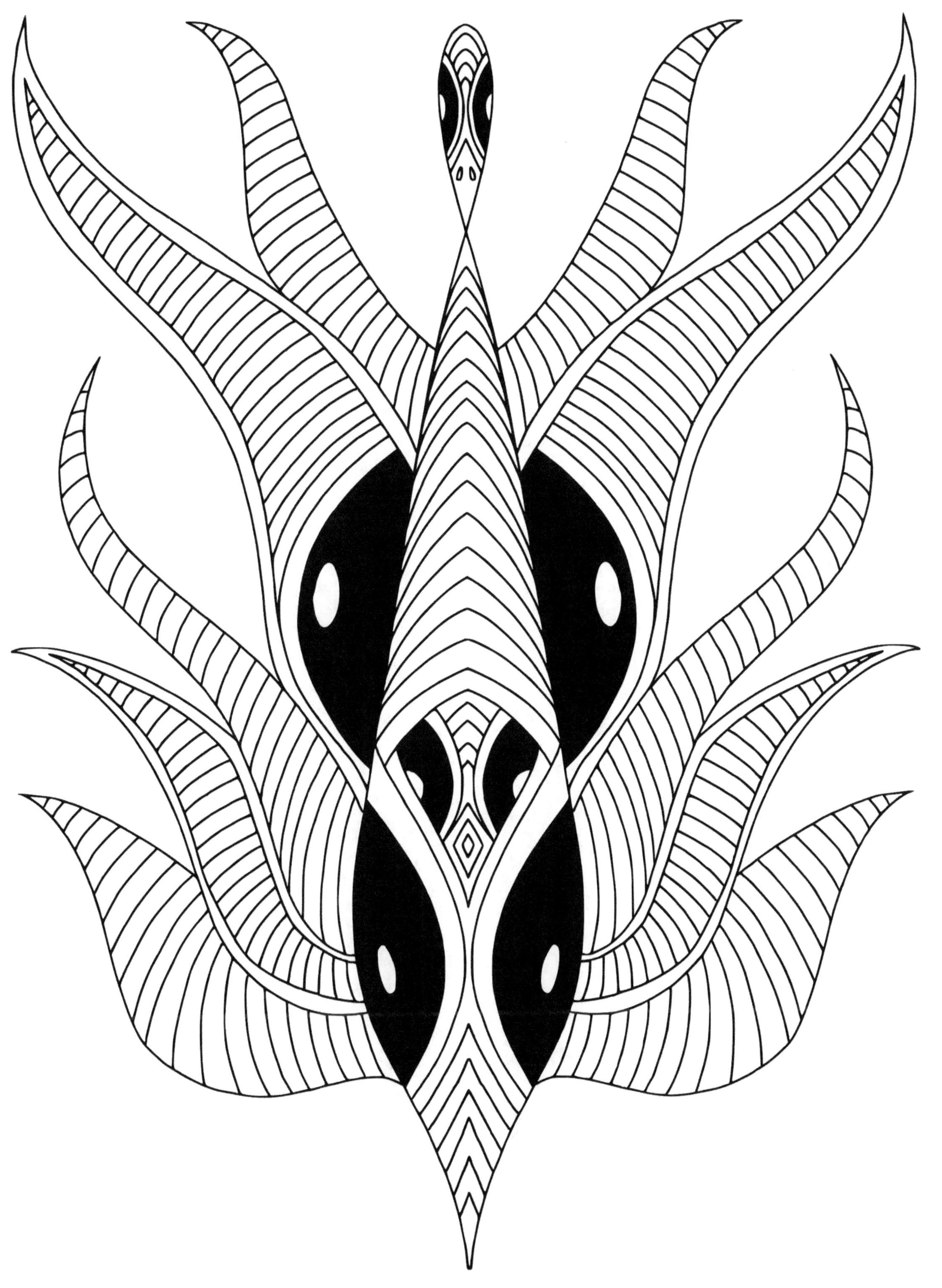

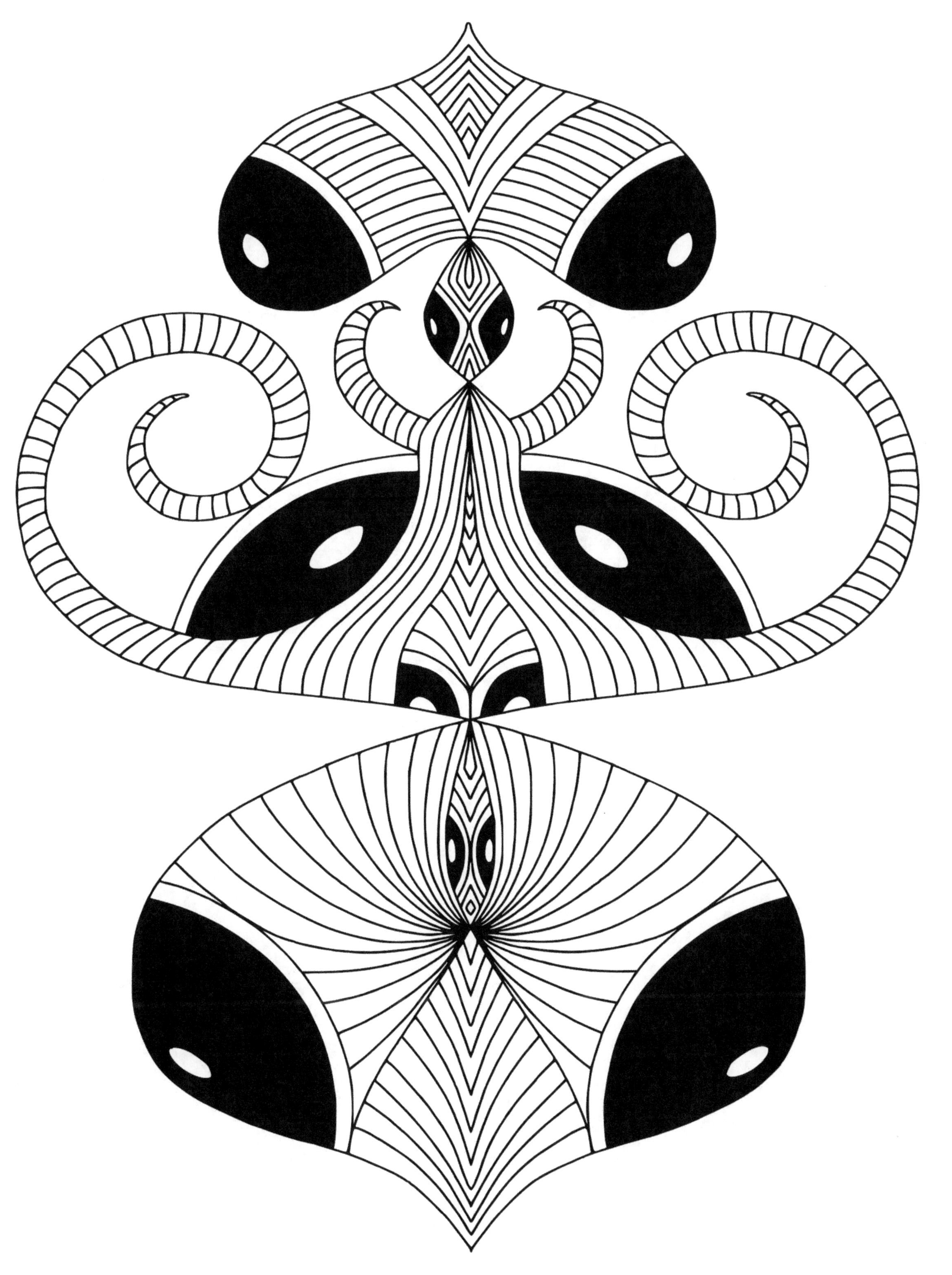

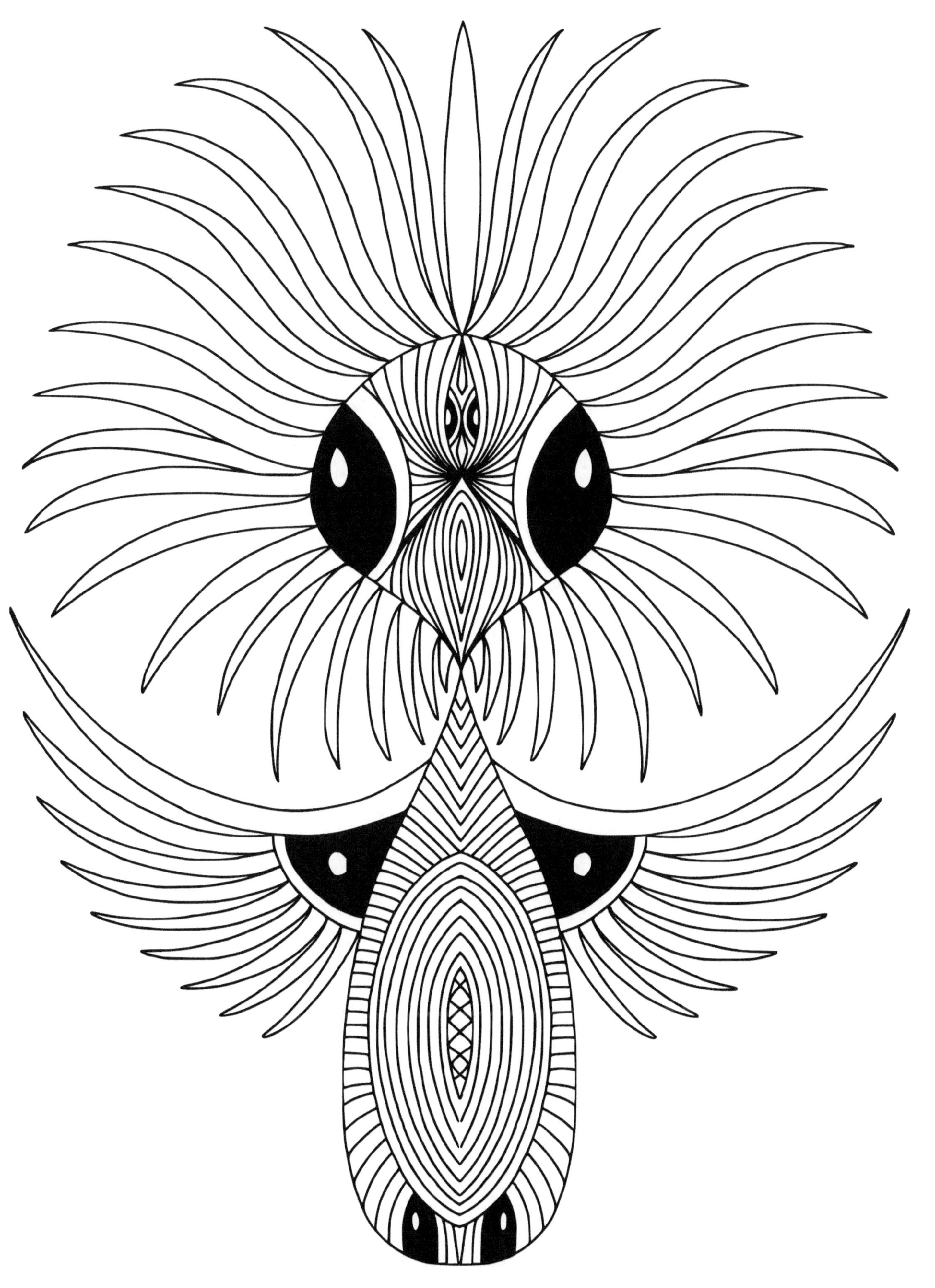

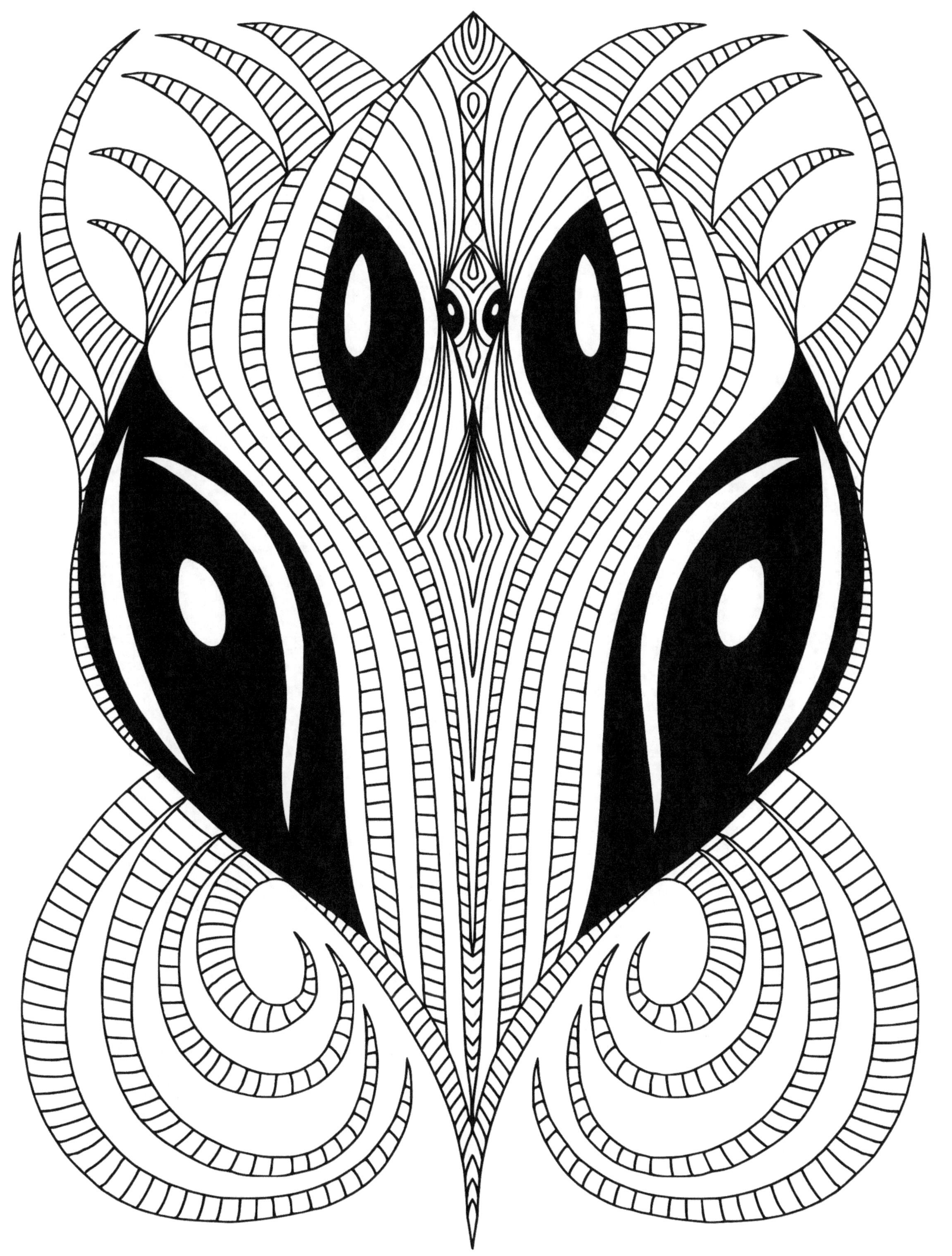

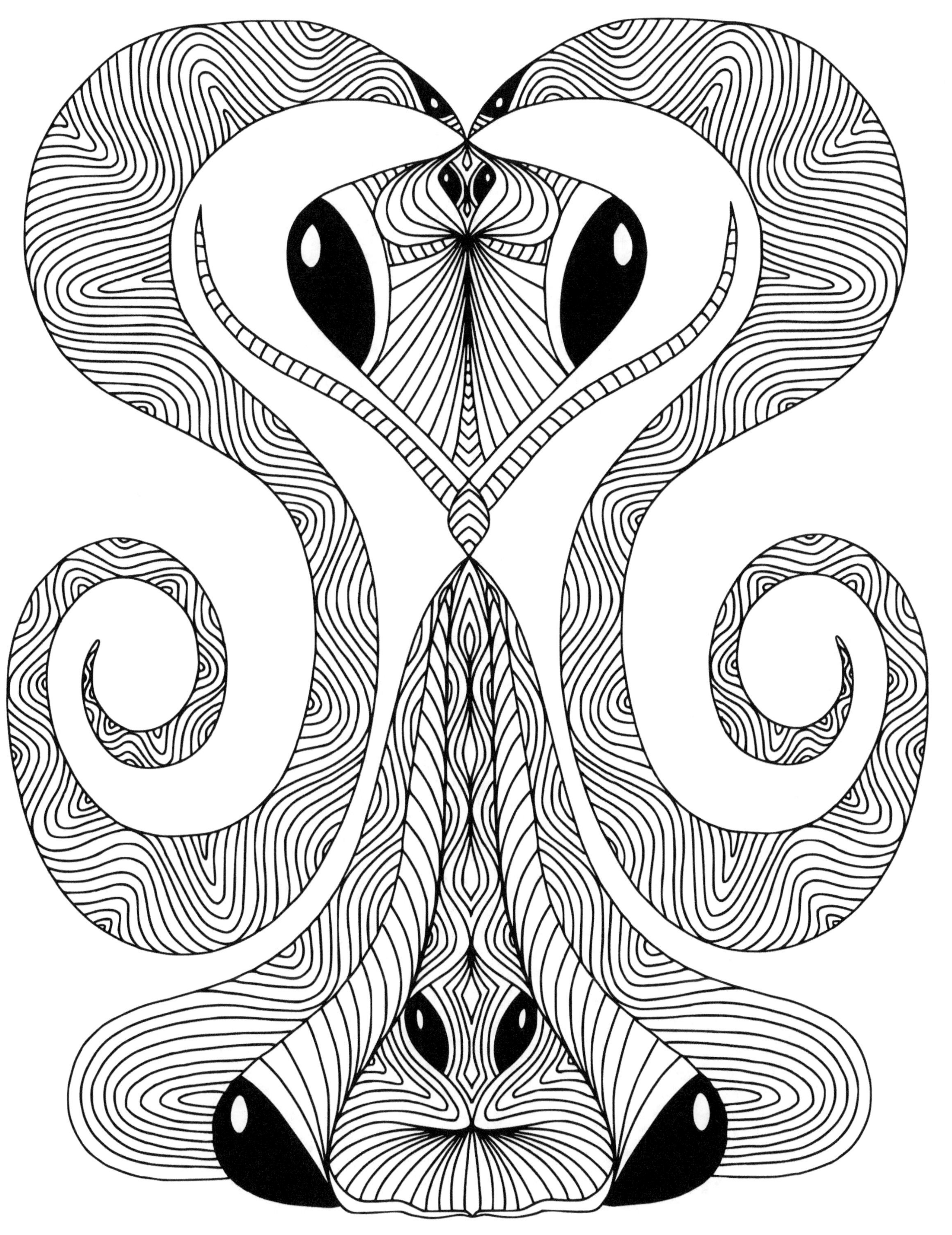

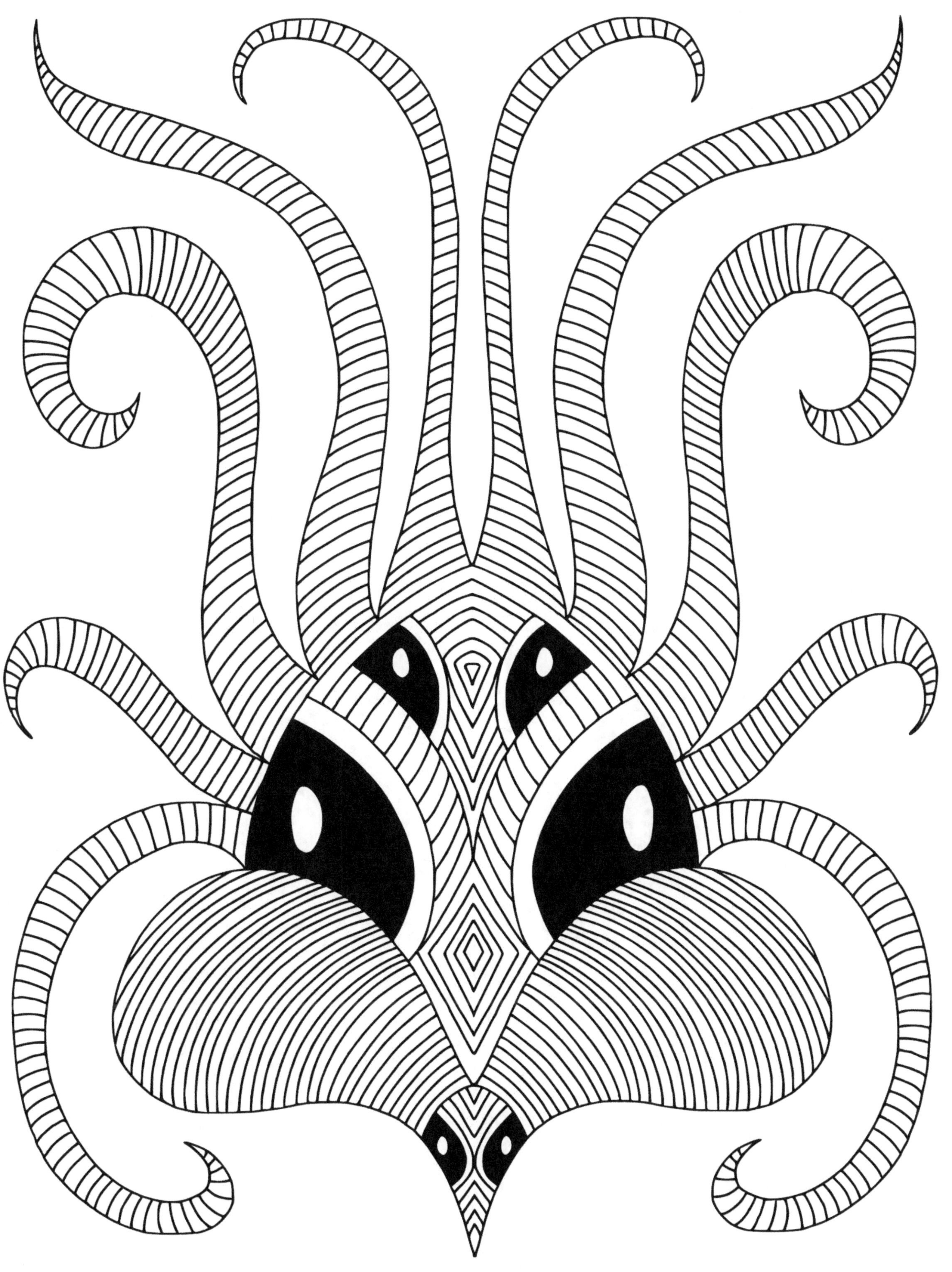

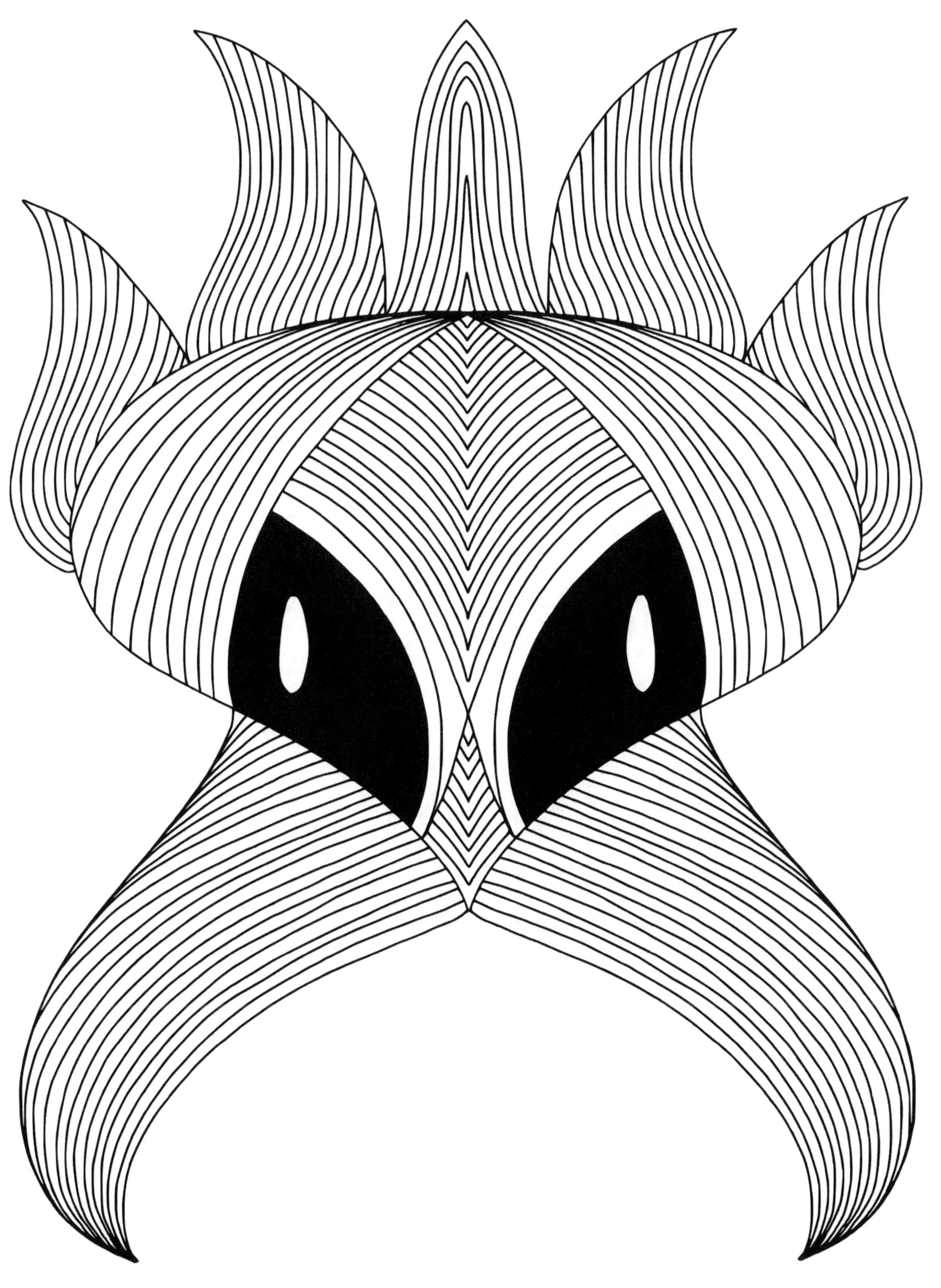

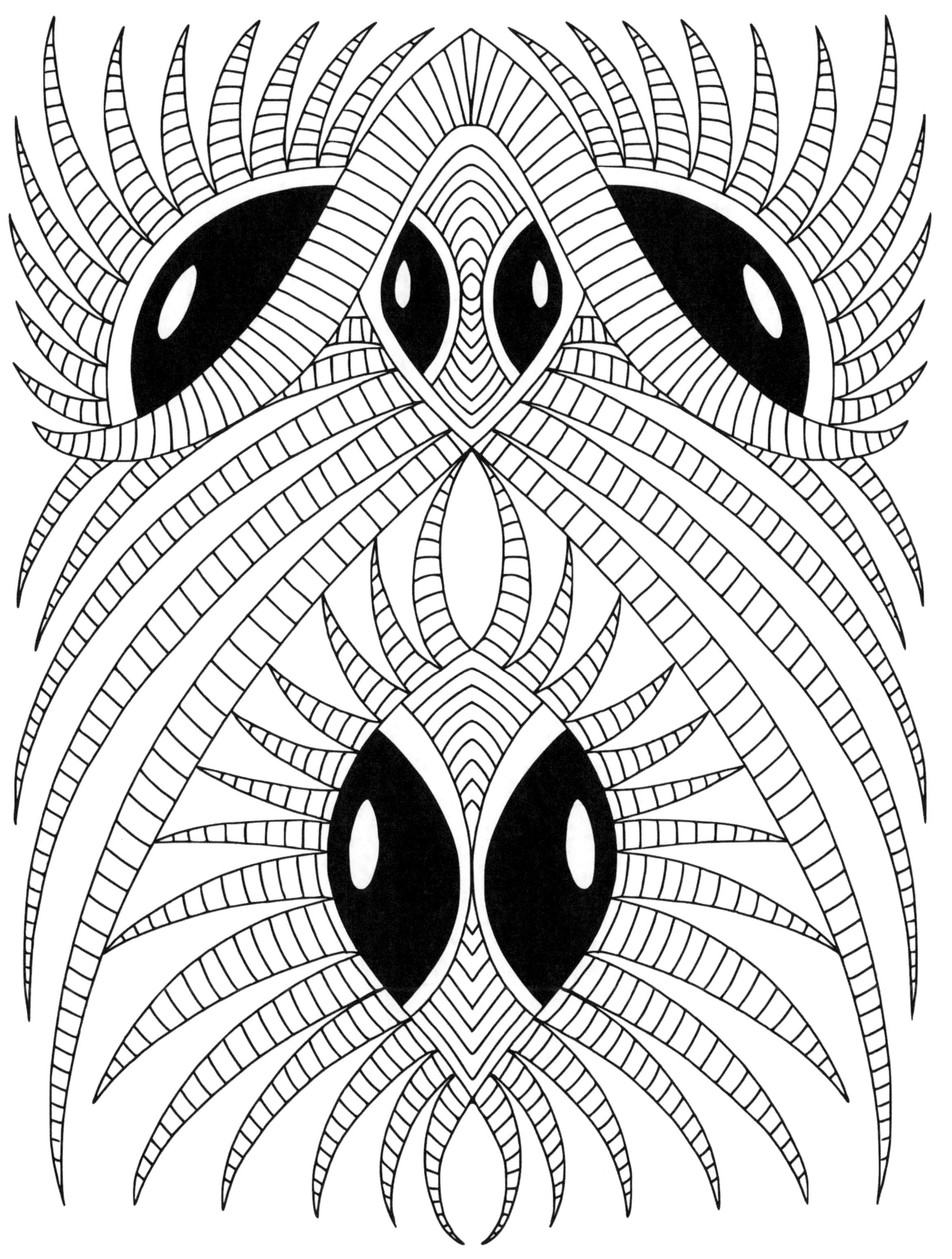

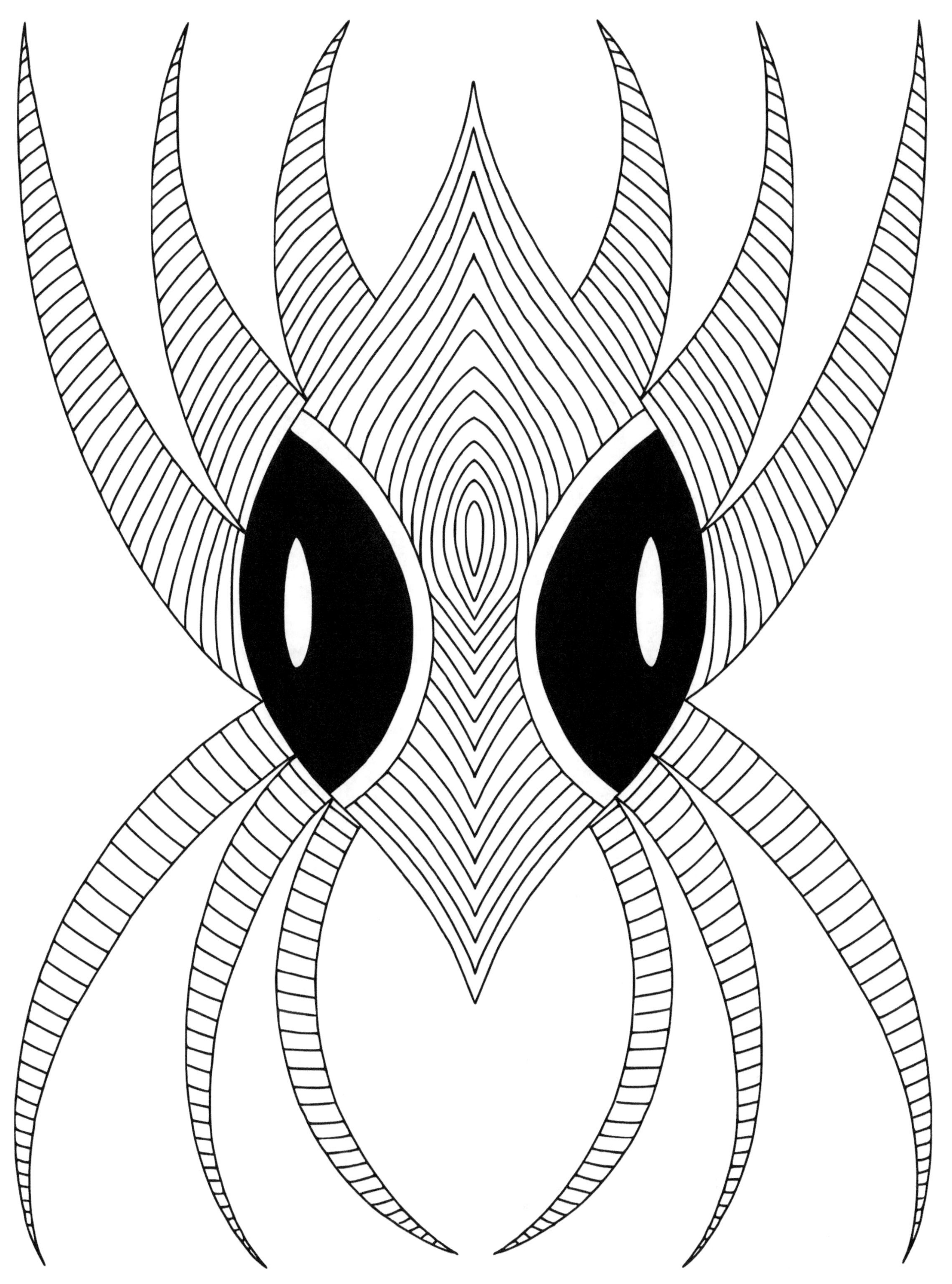

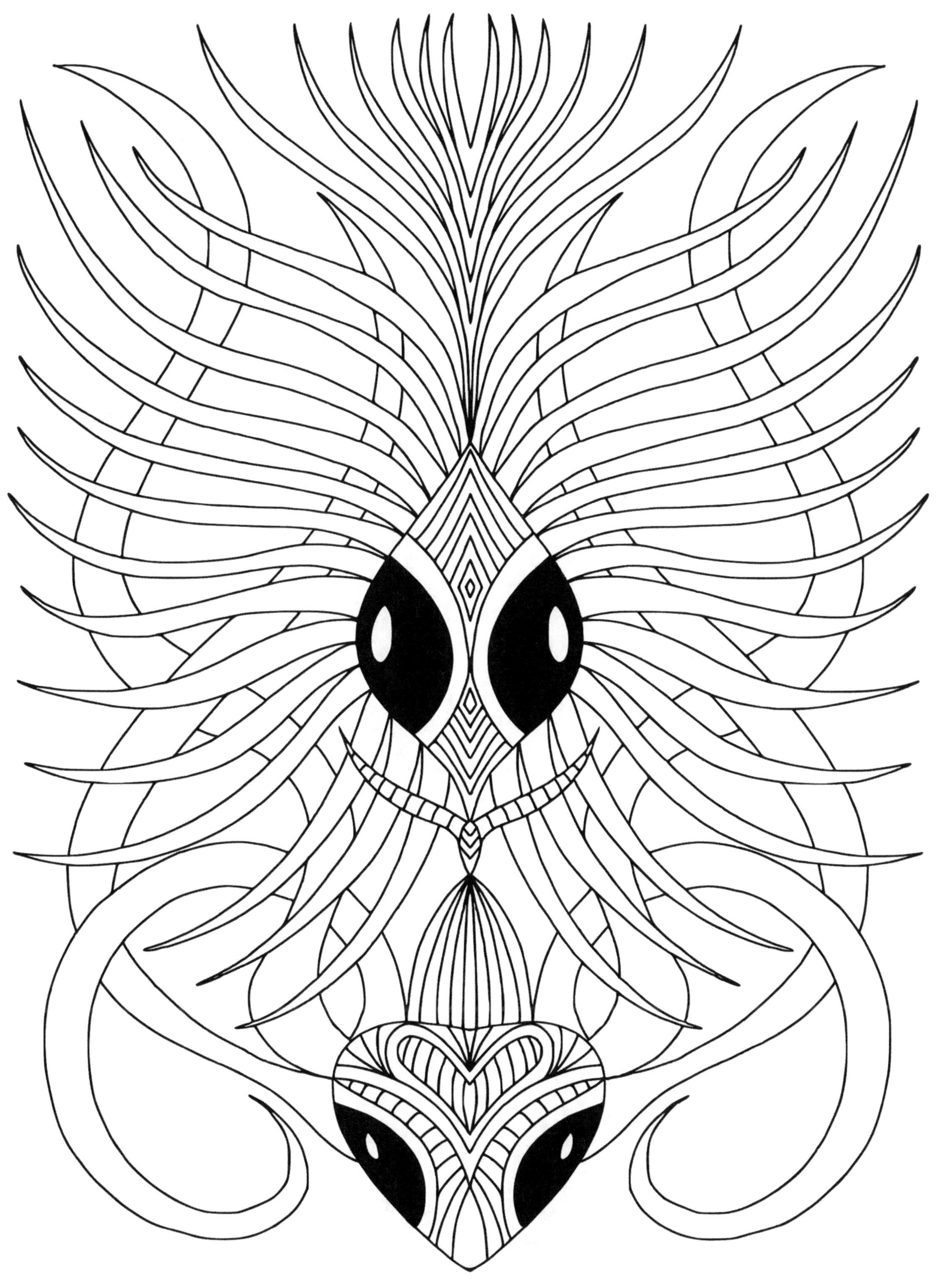

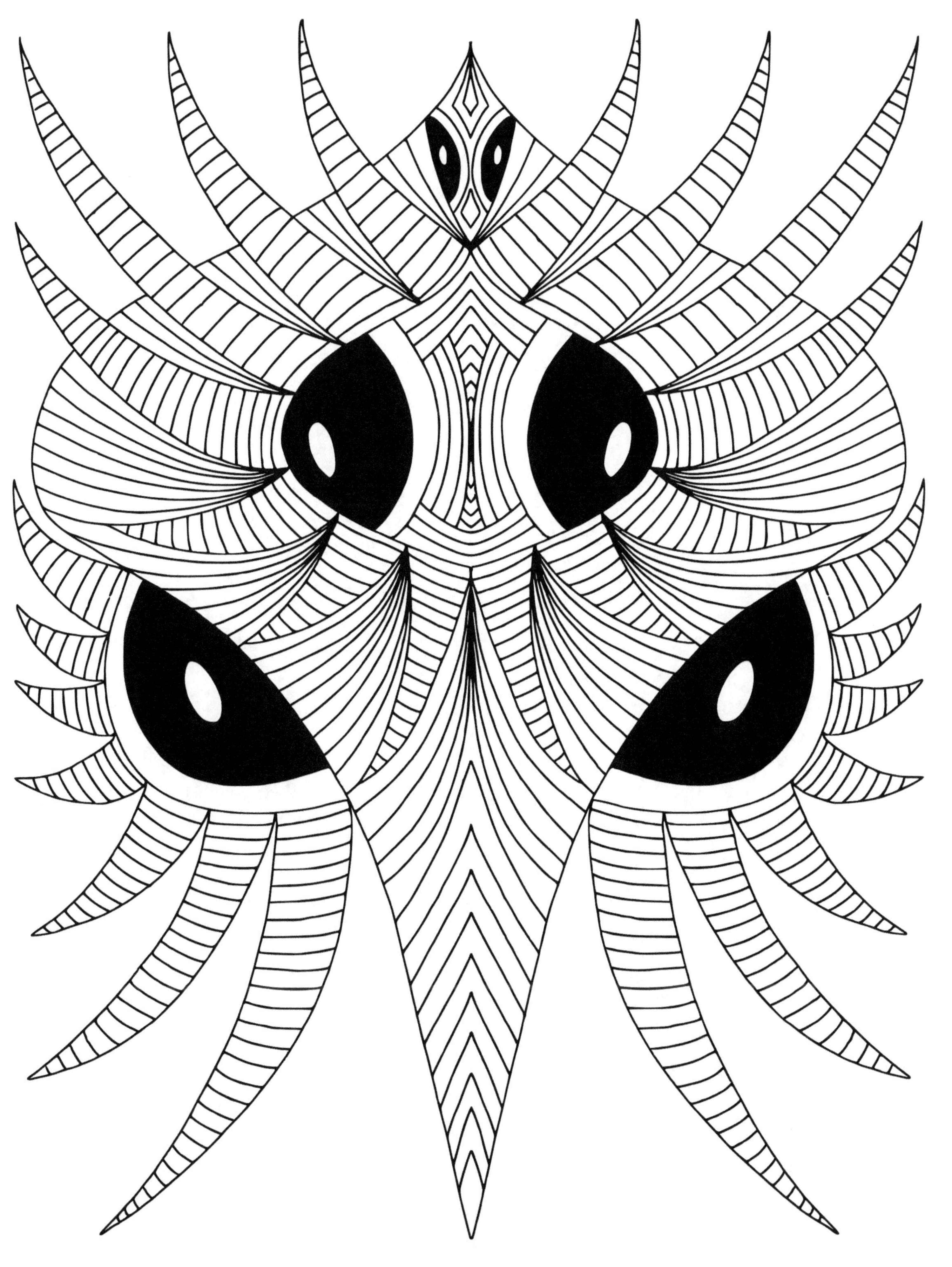

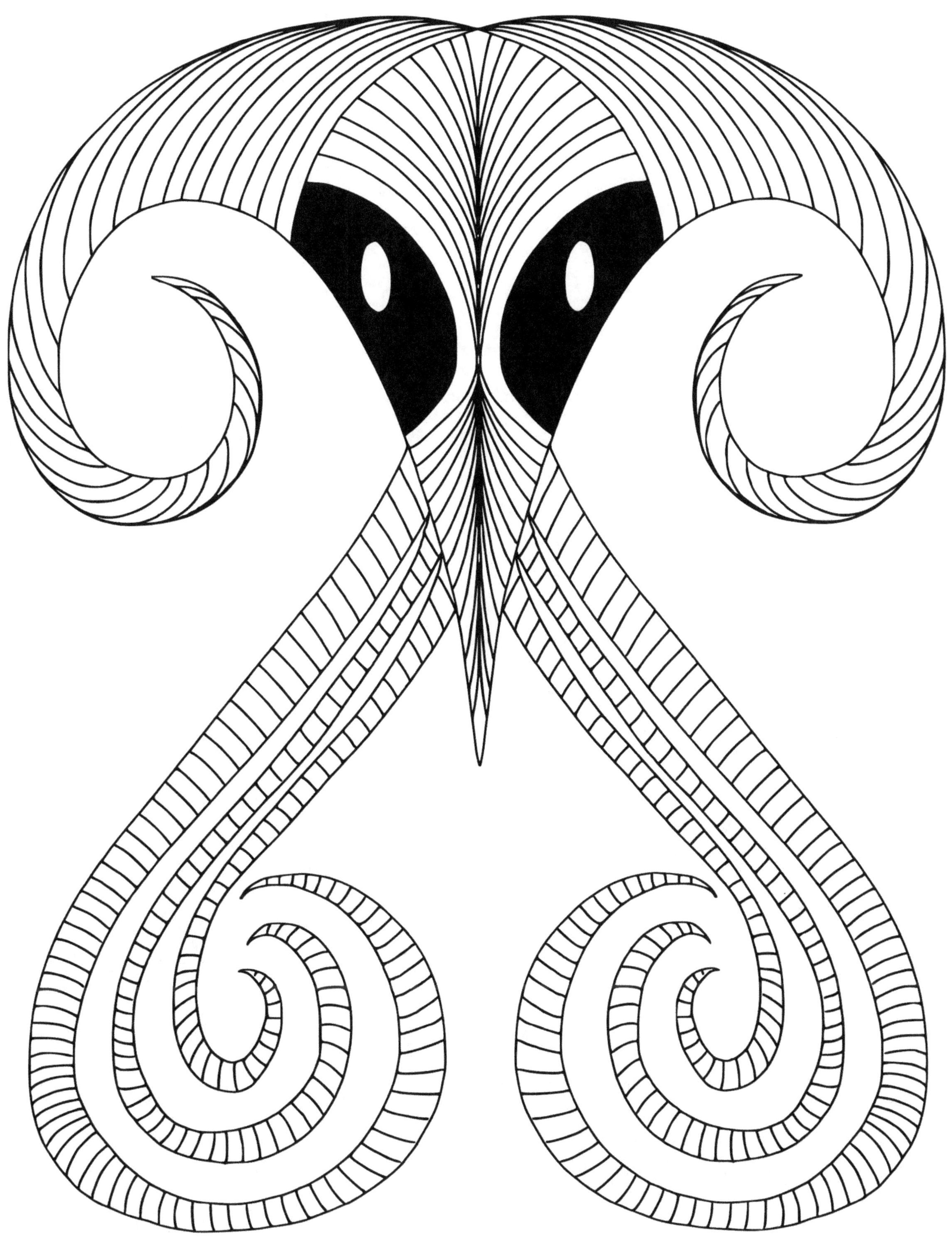

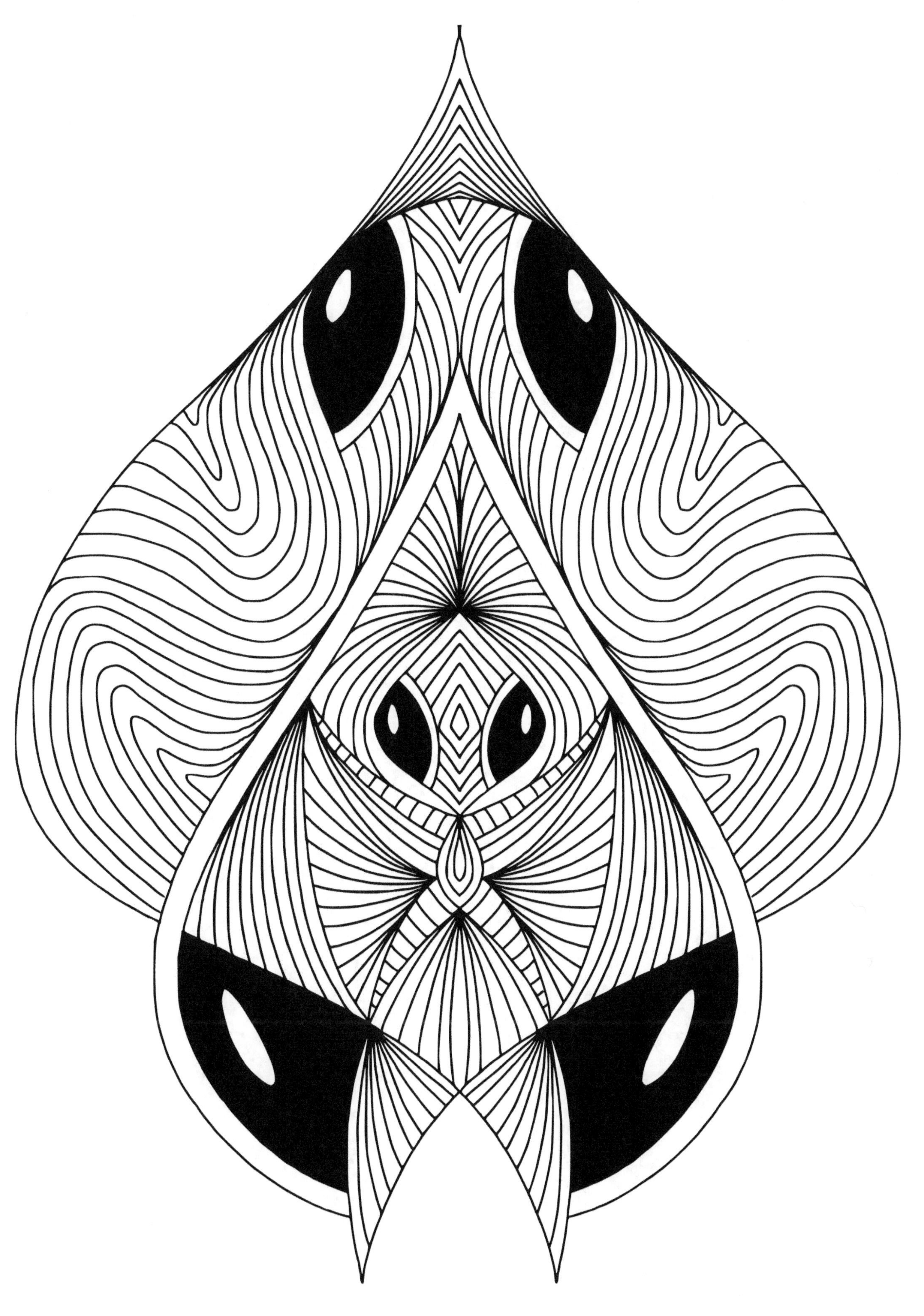

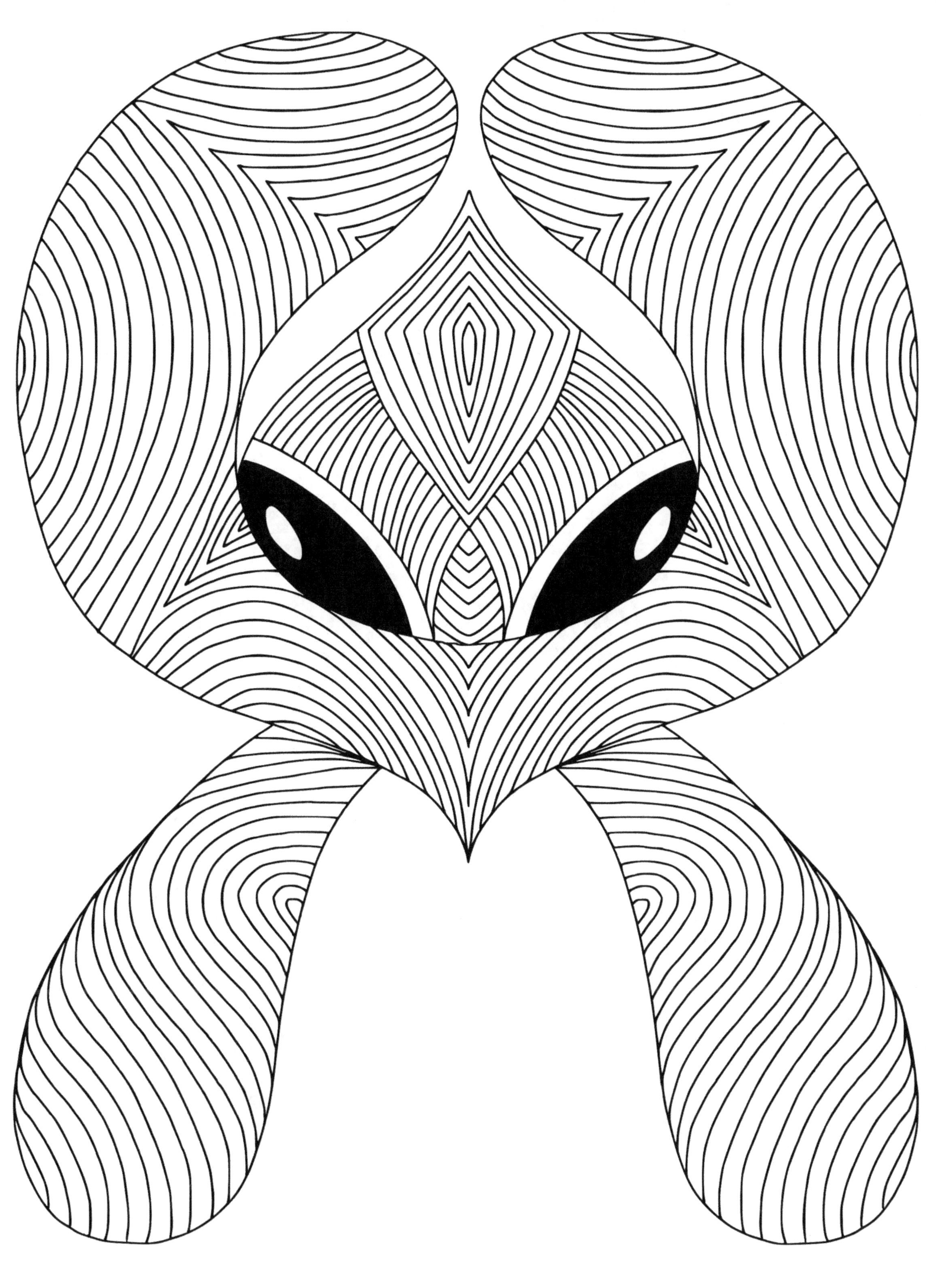

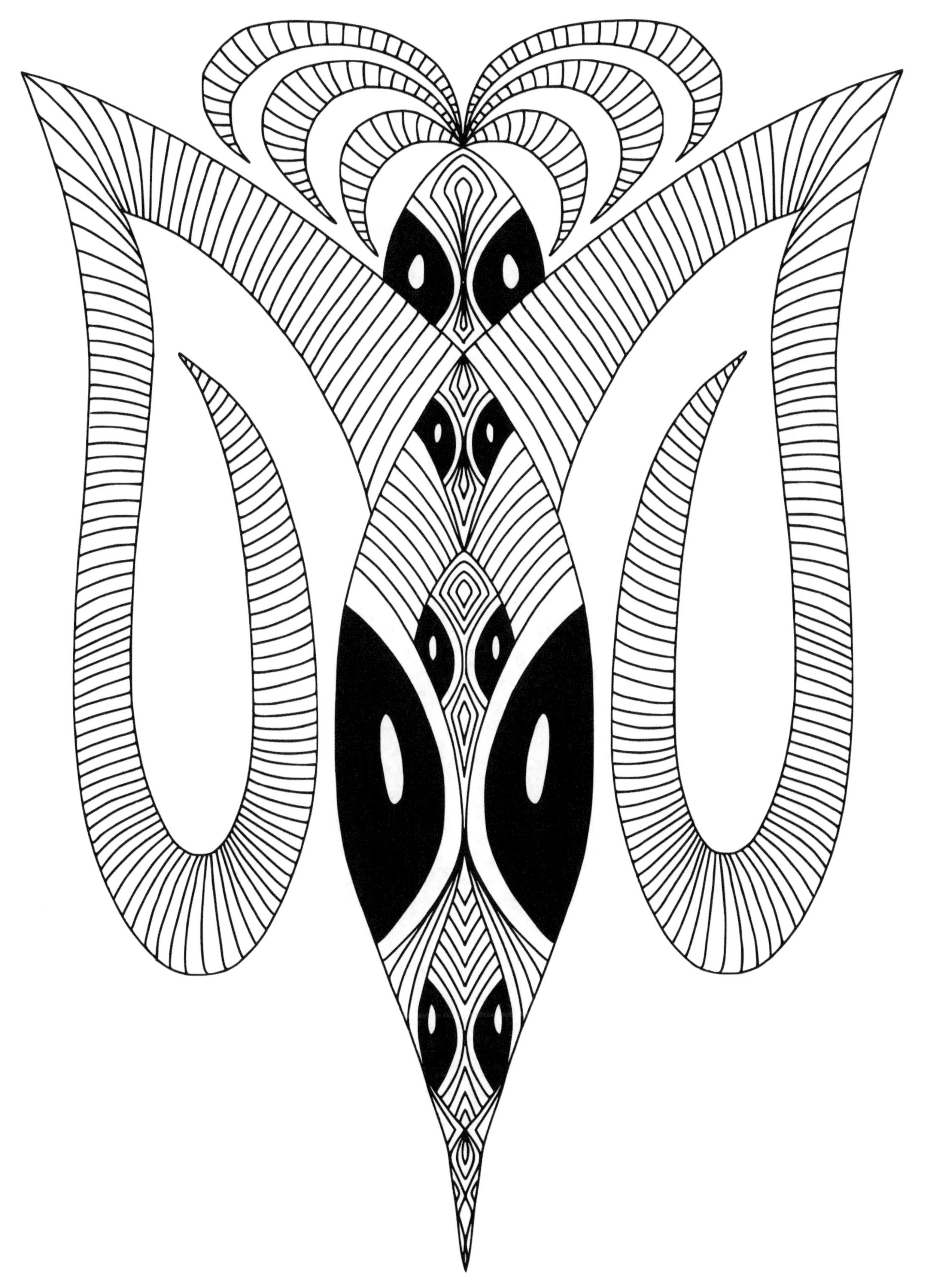

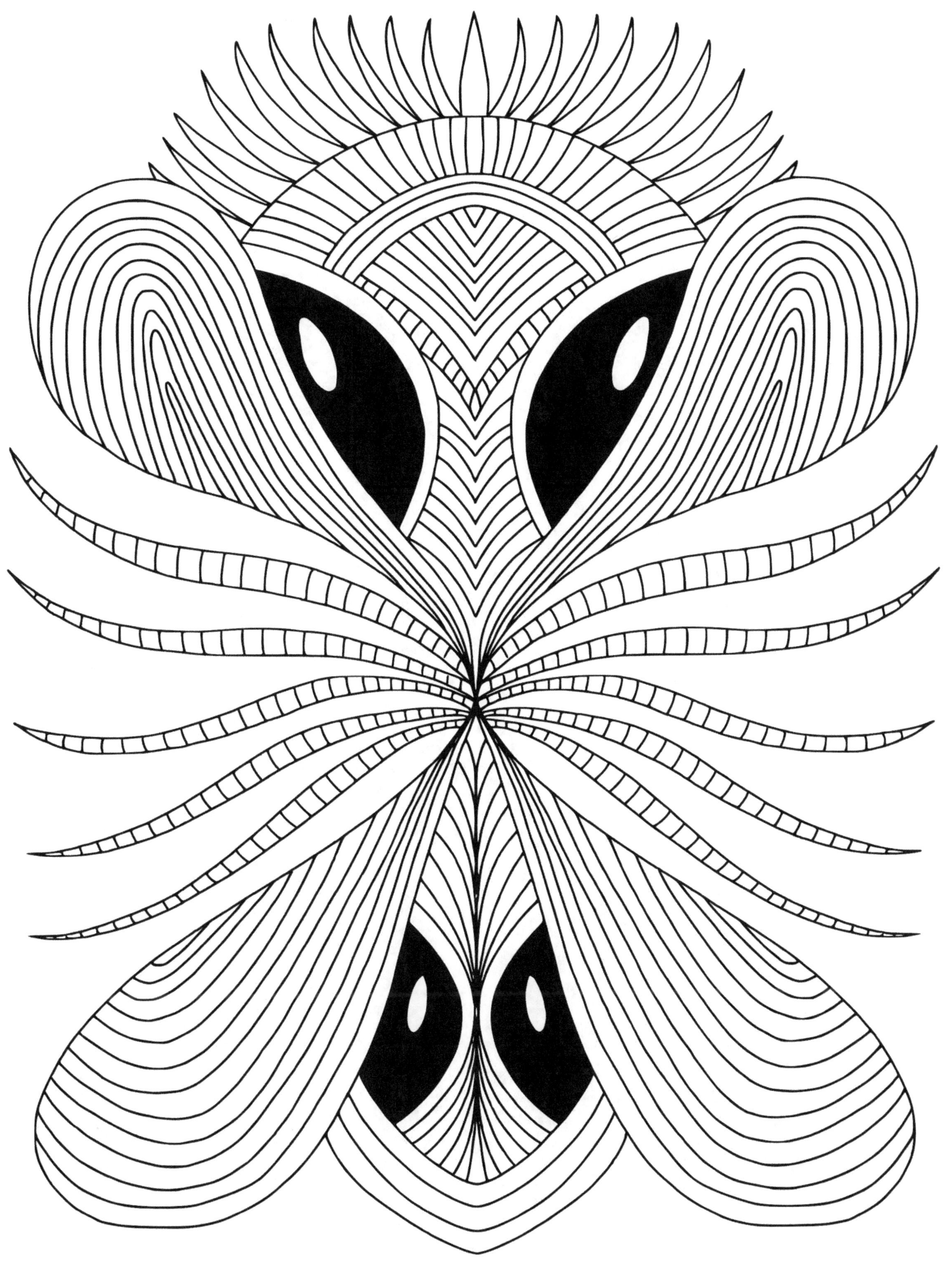

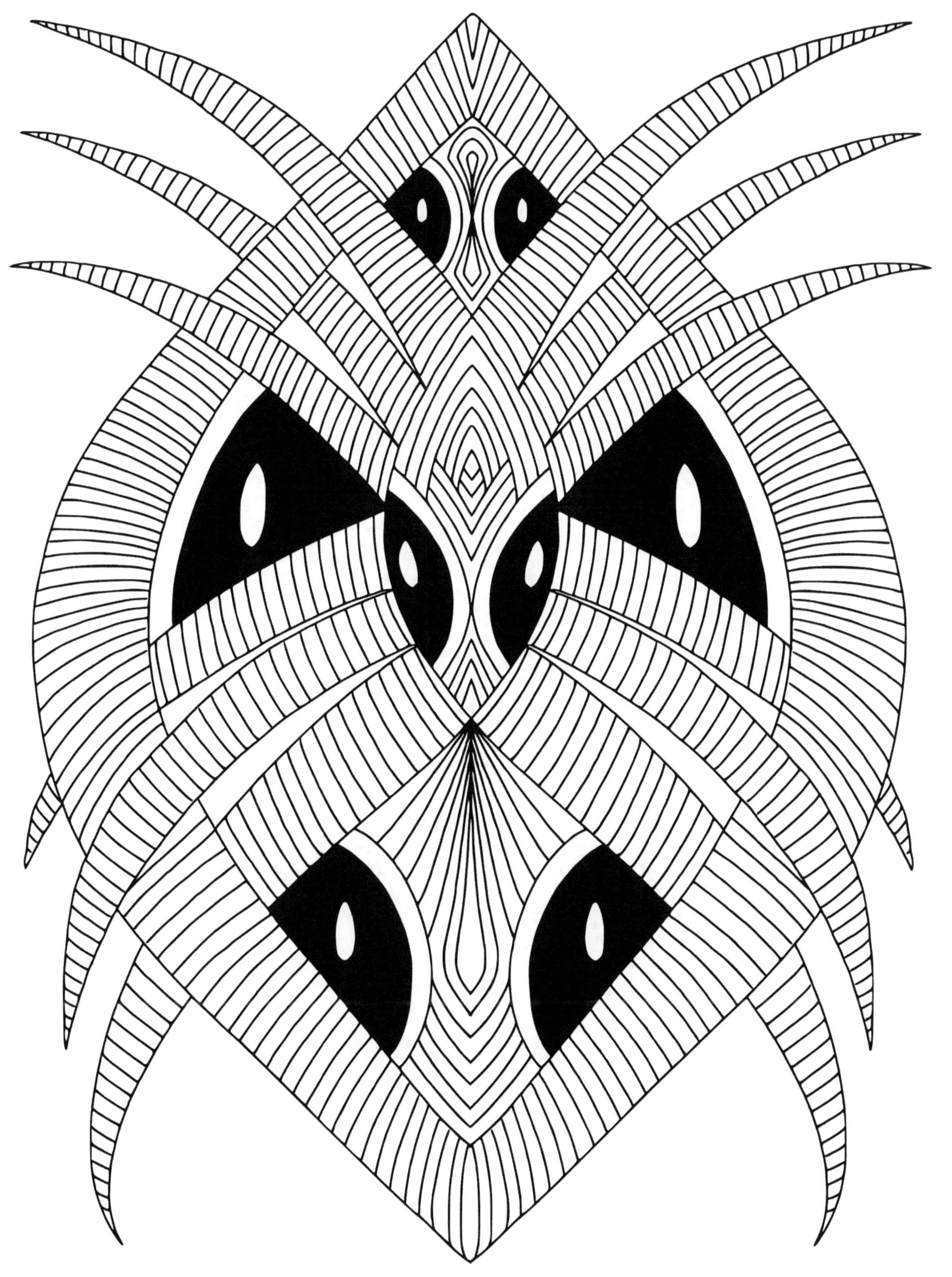

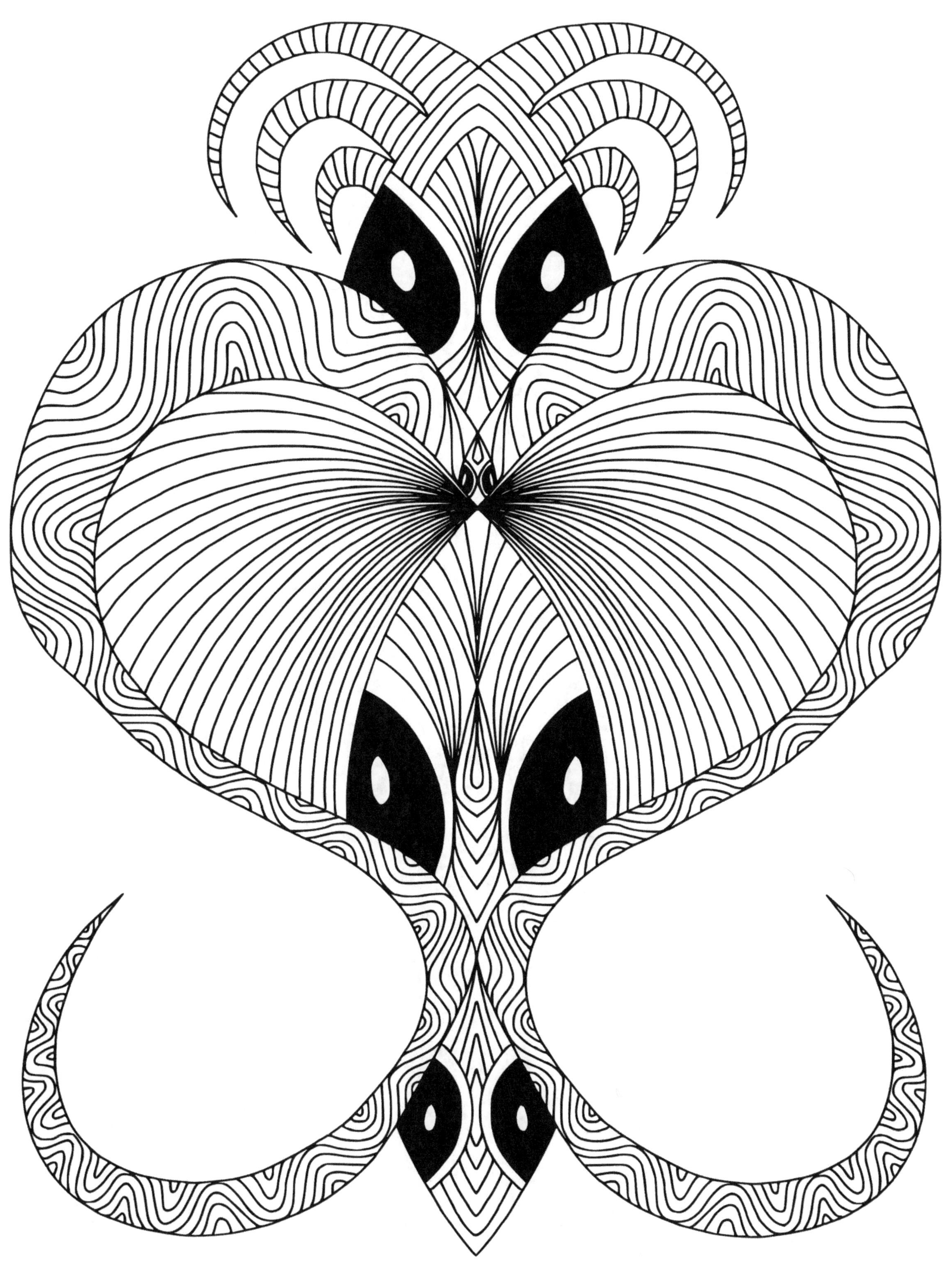

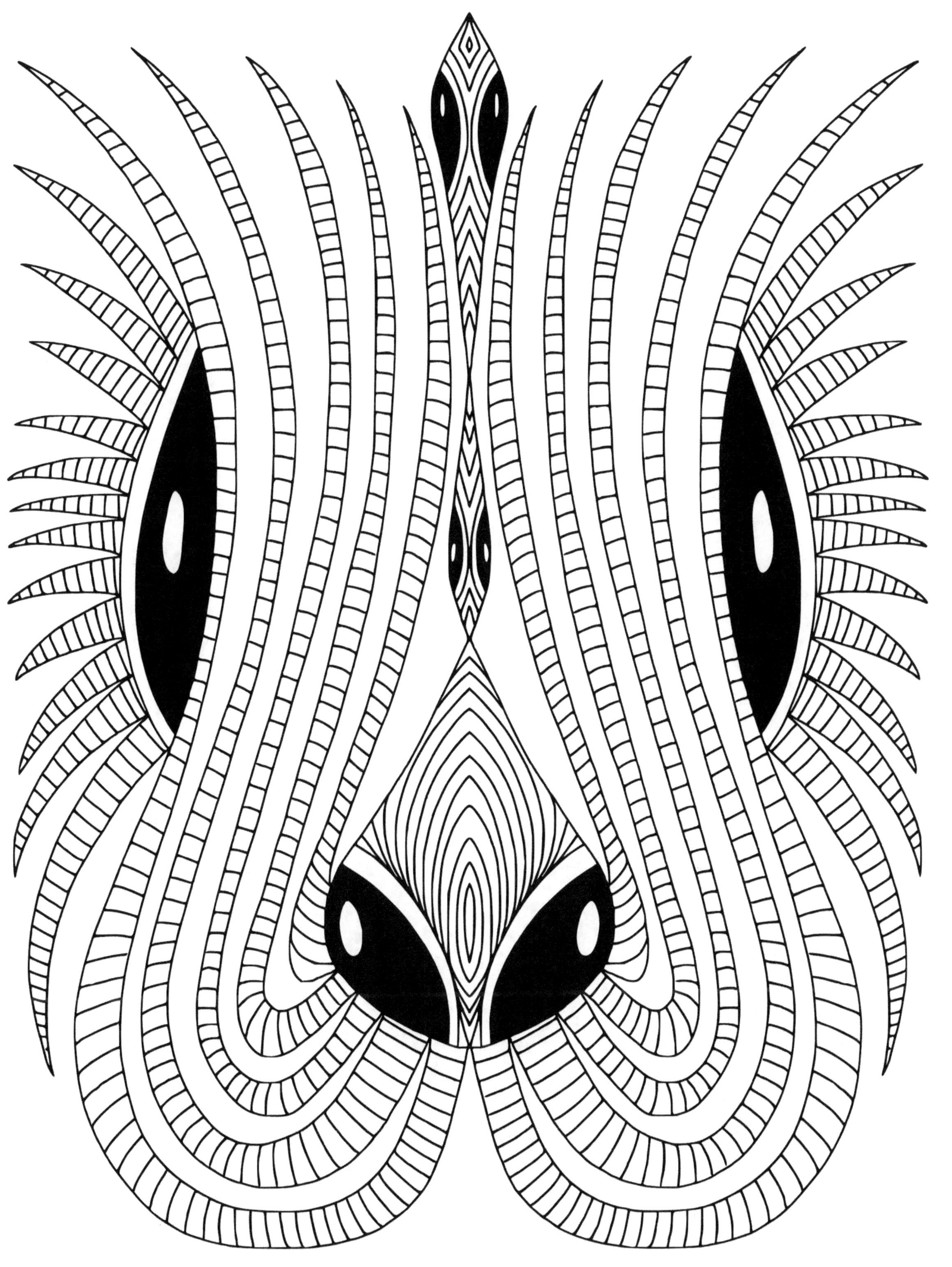

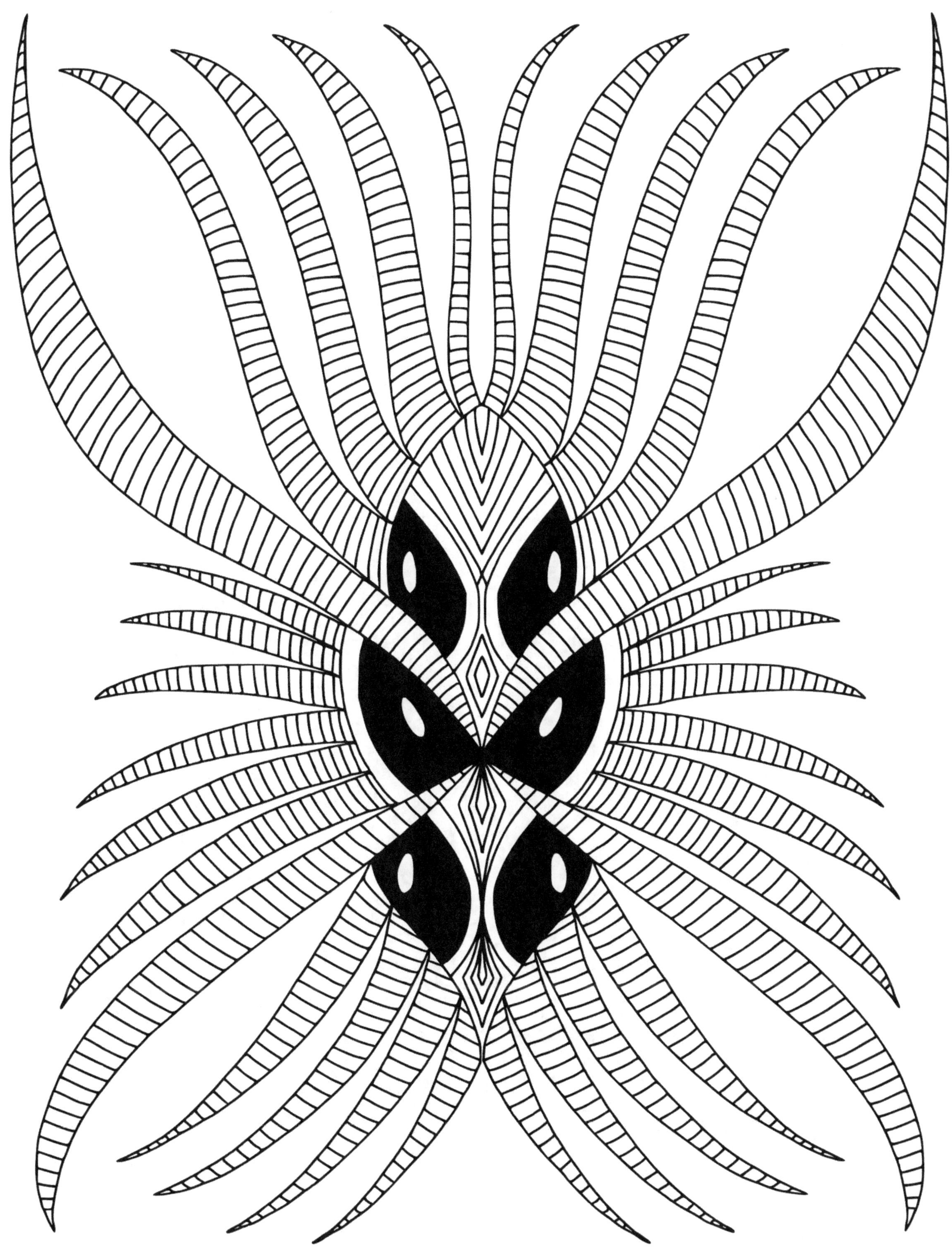

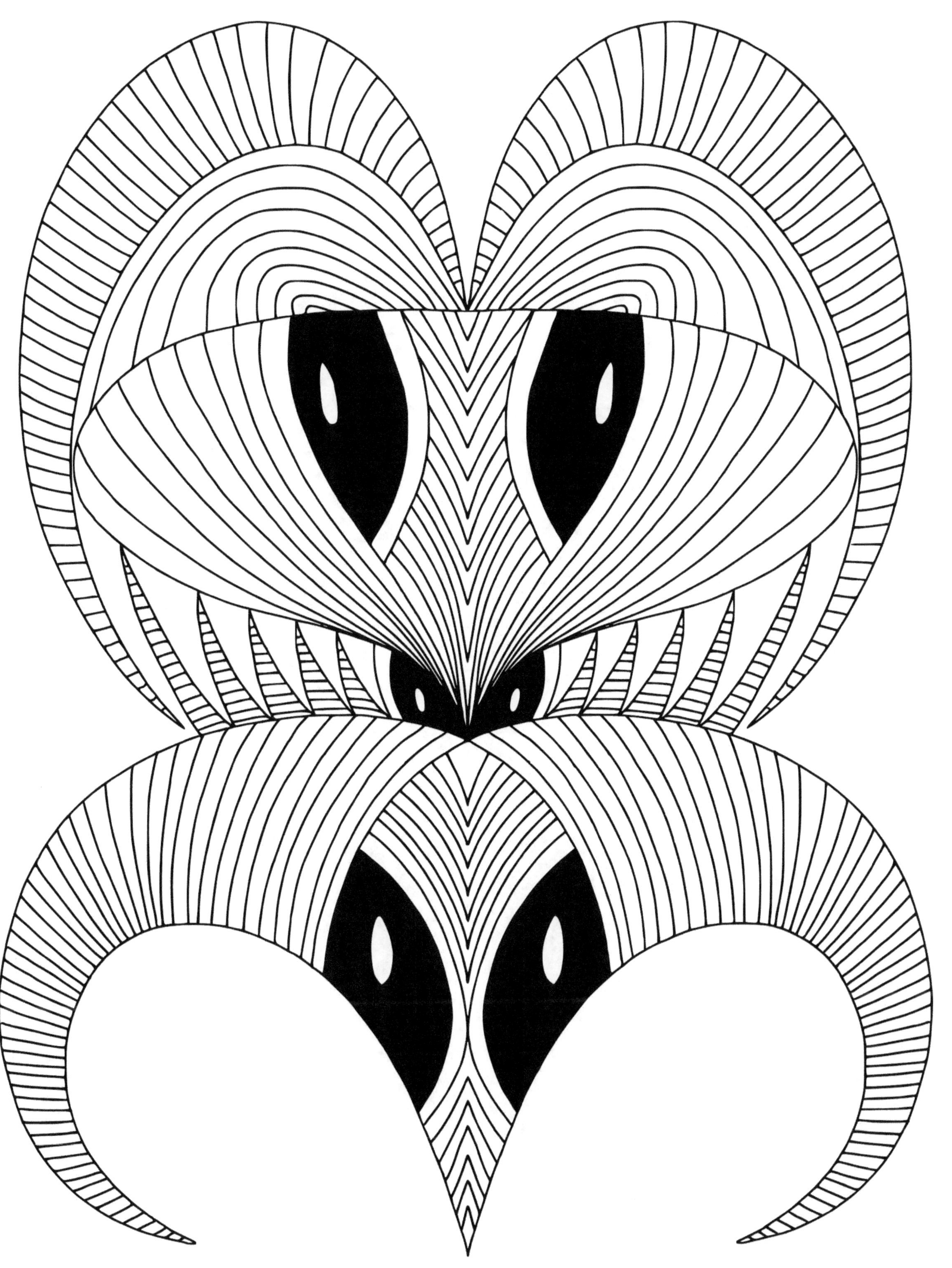

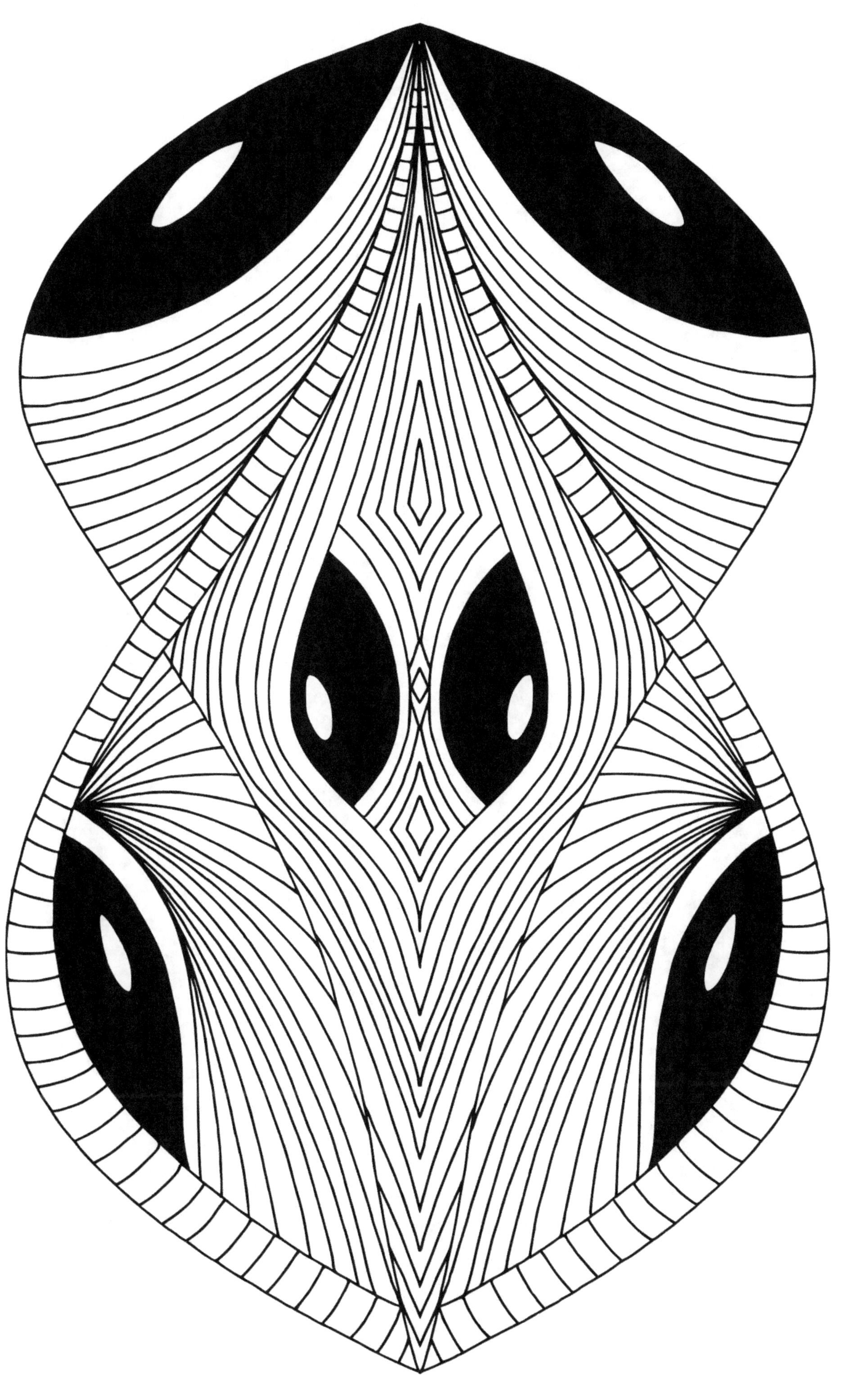

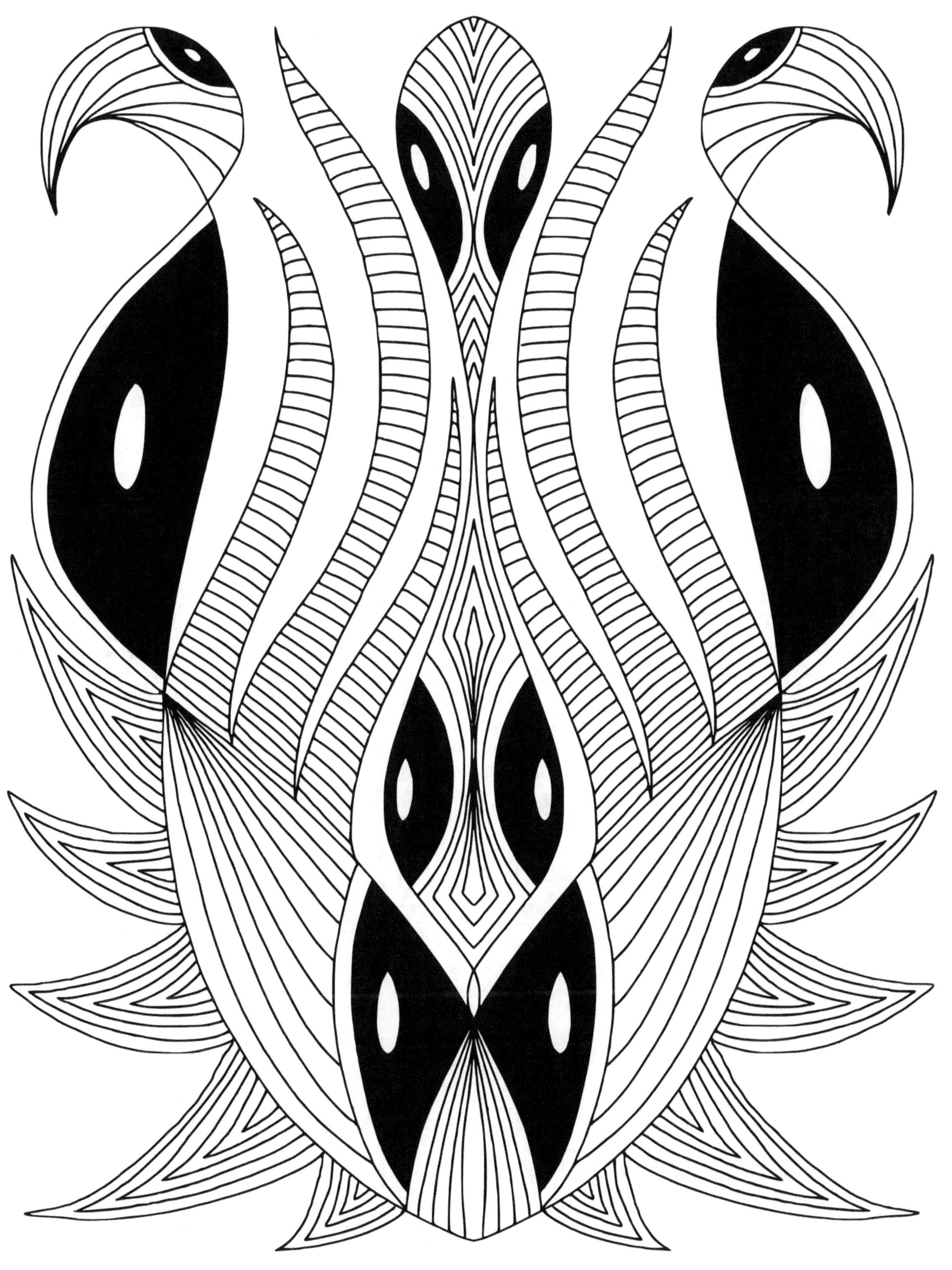

Bonus Upside Down versions......

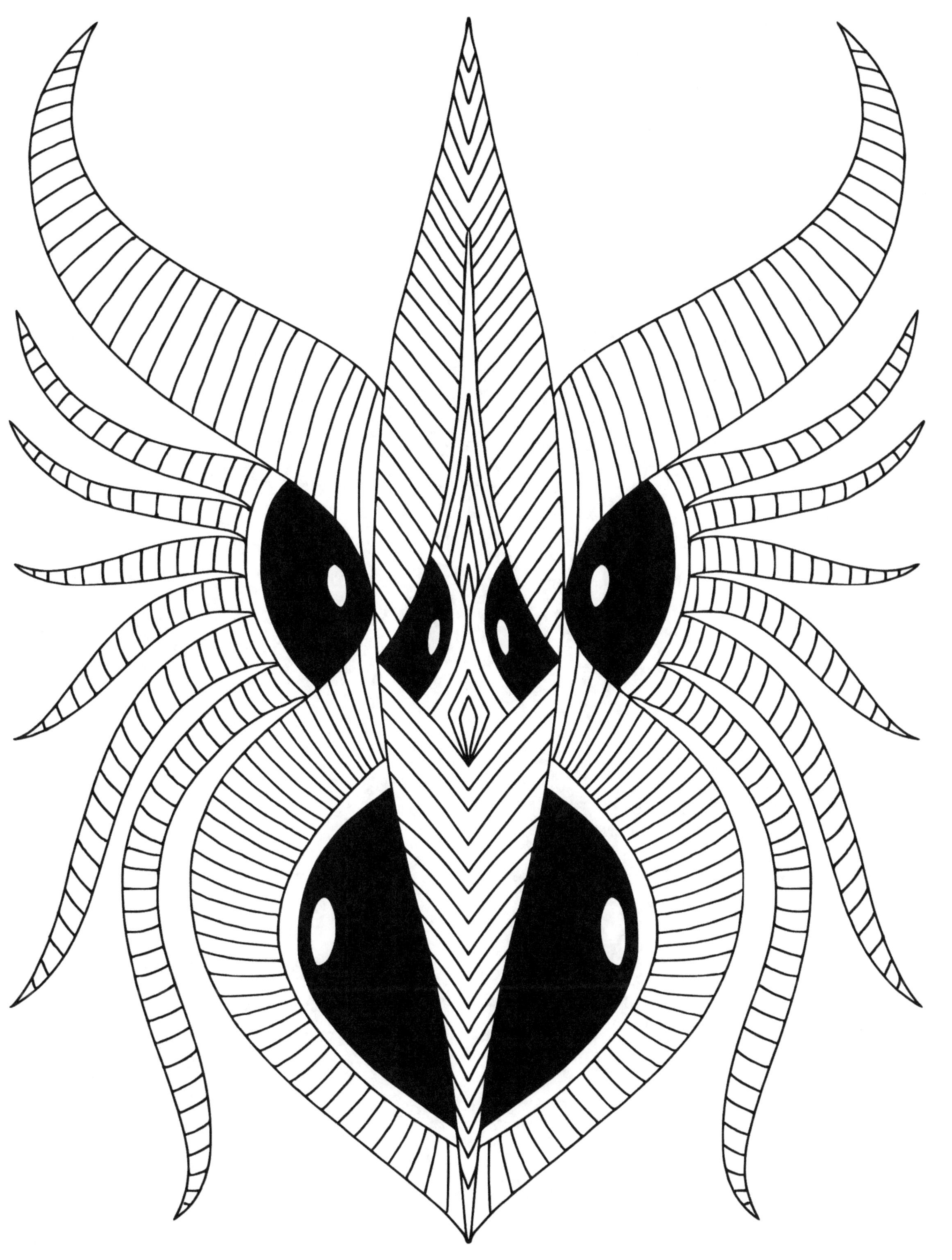

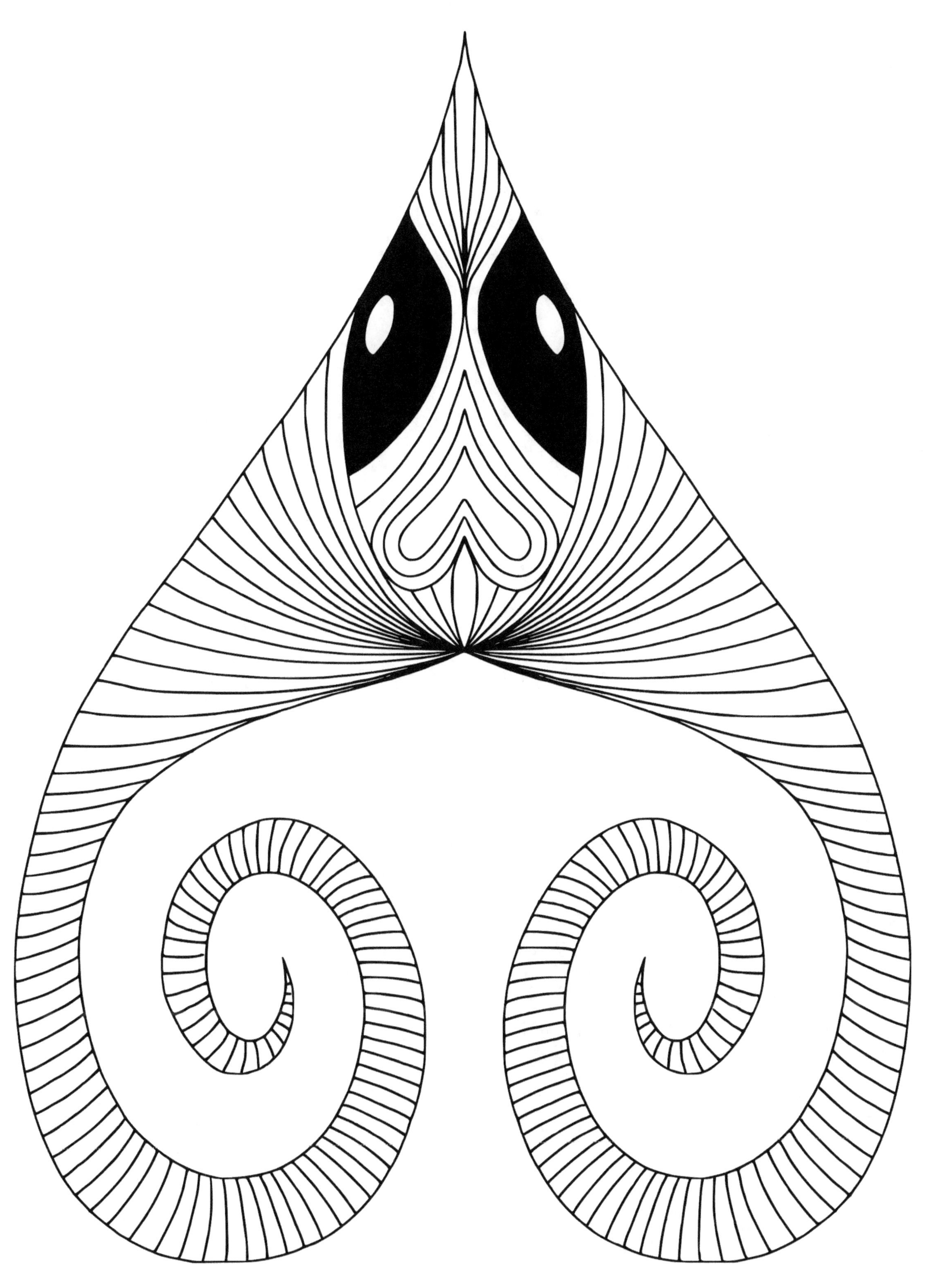

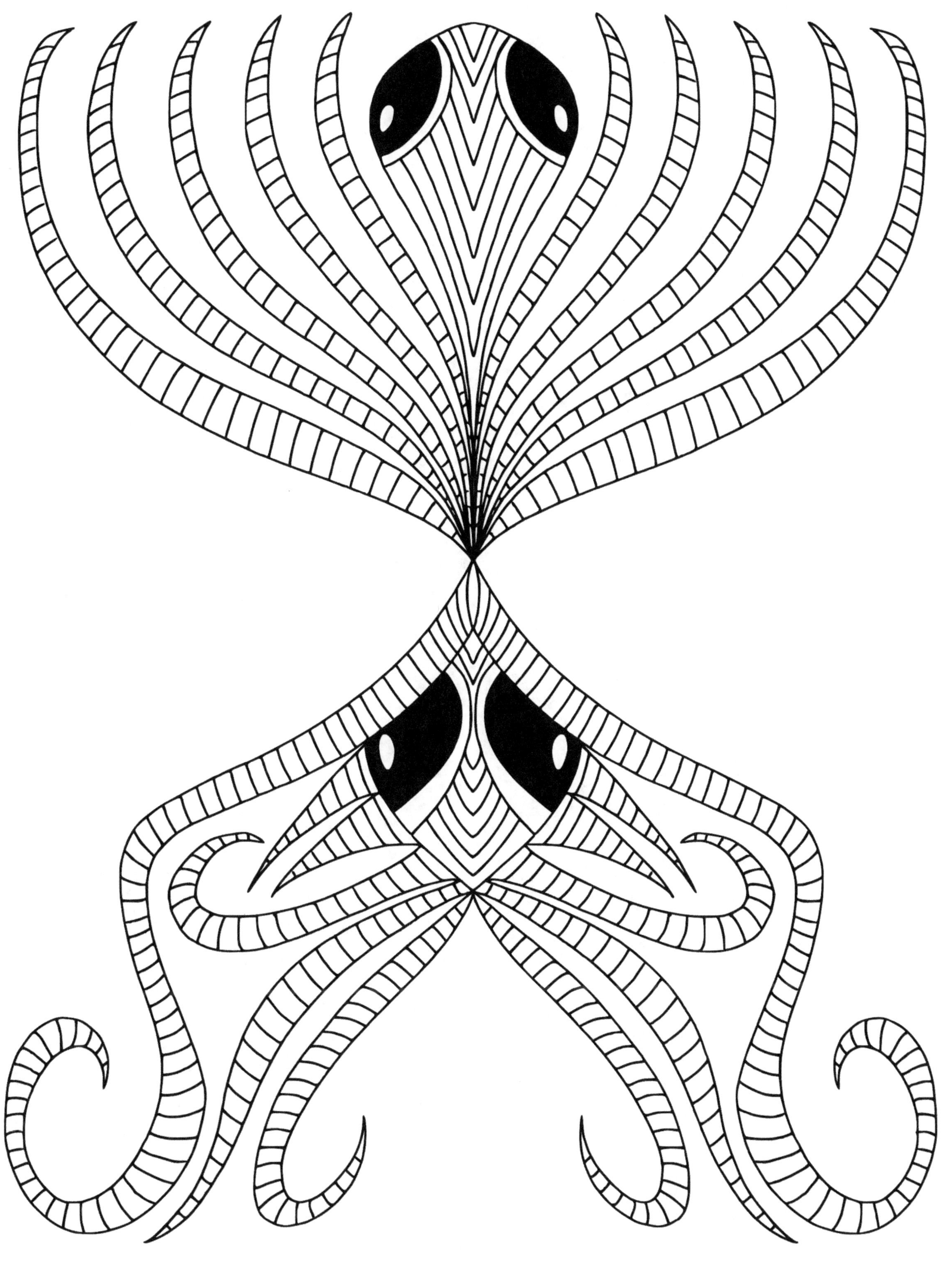

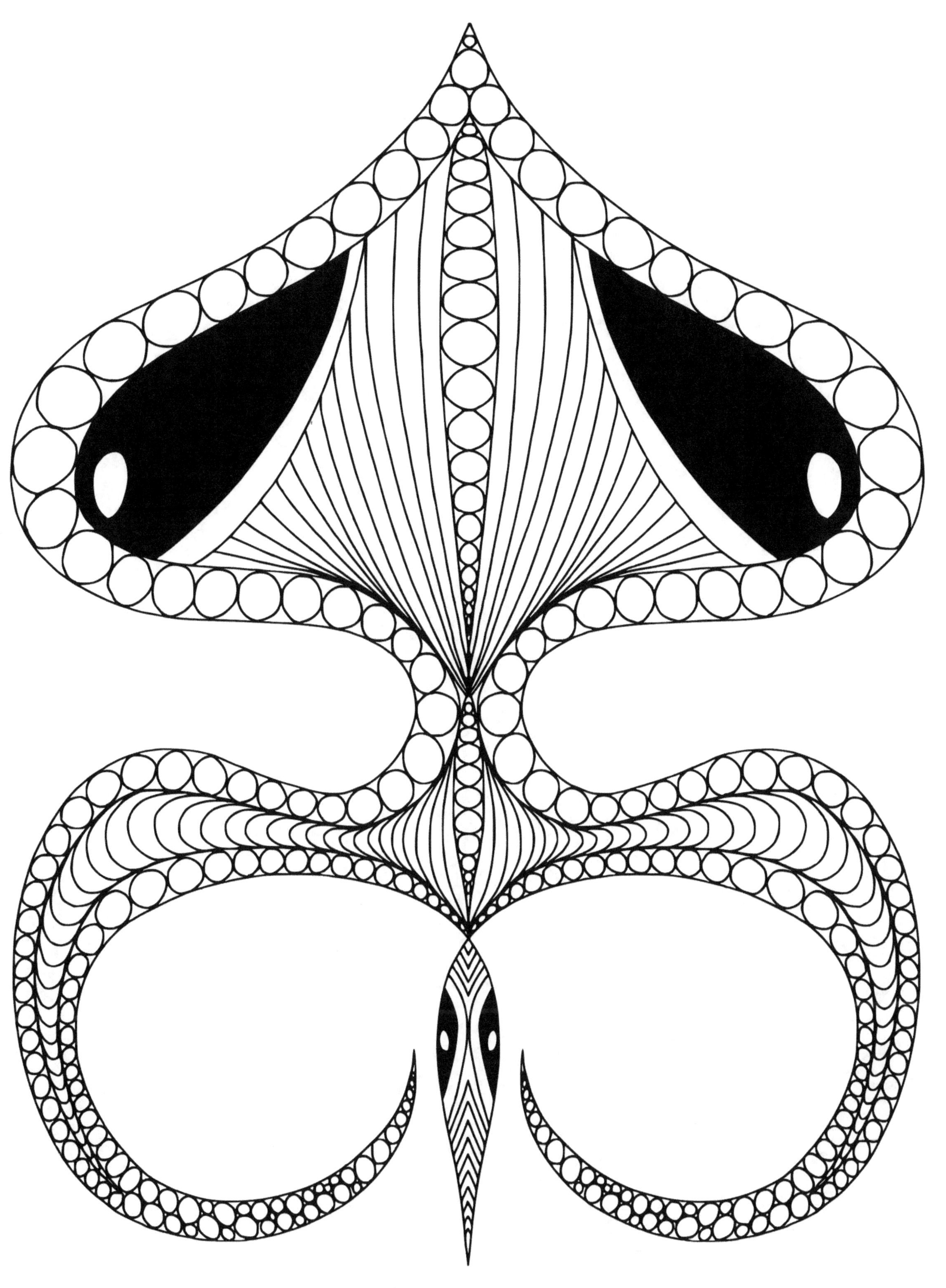

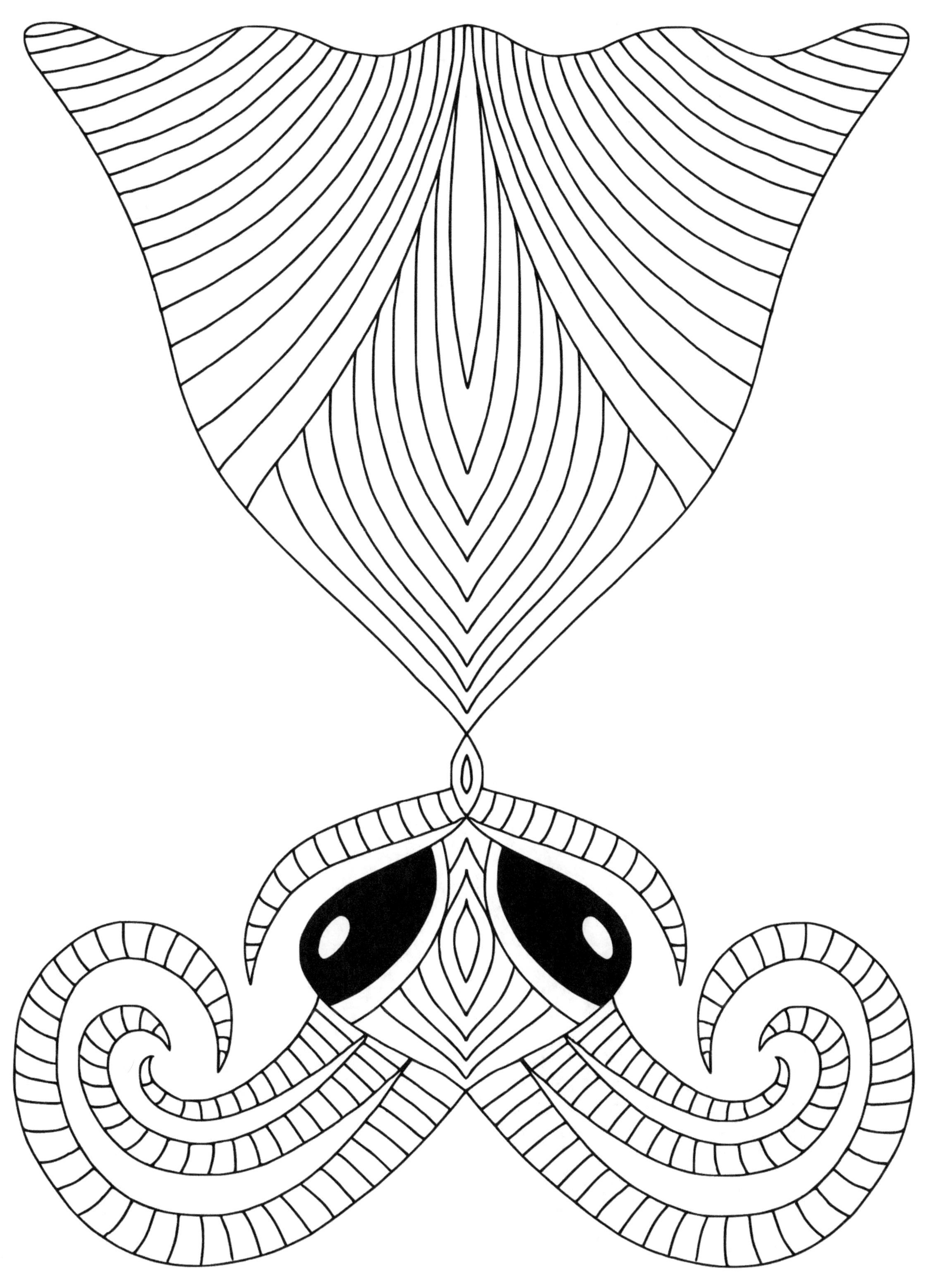

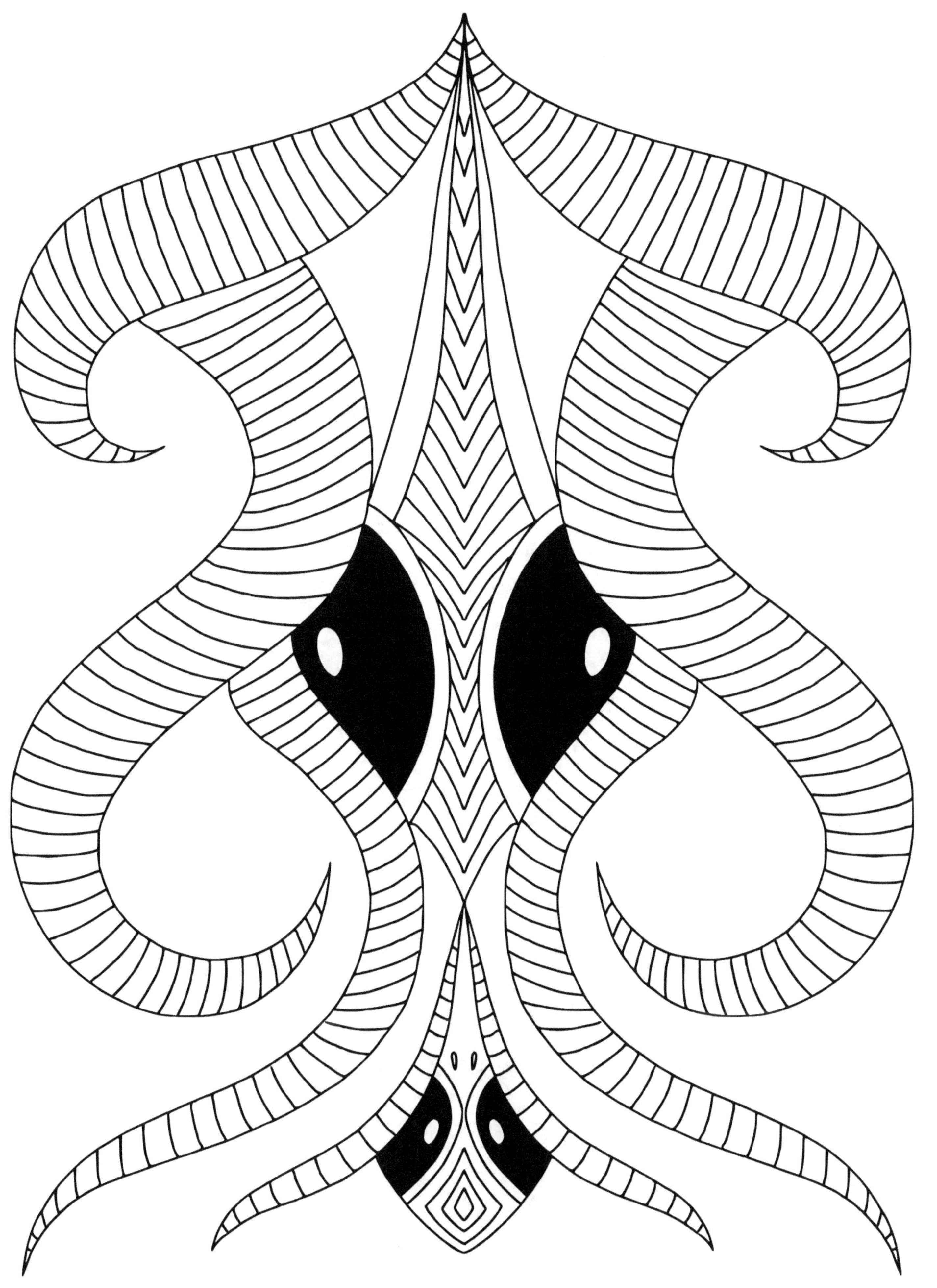

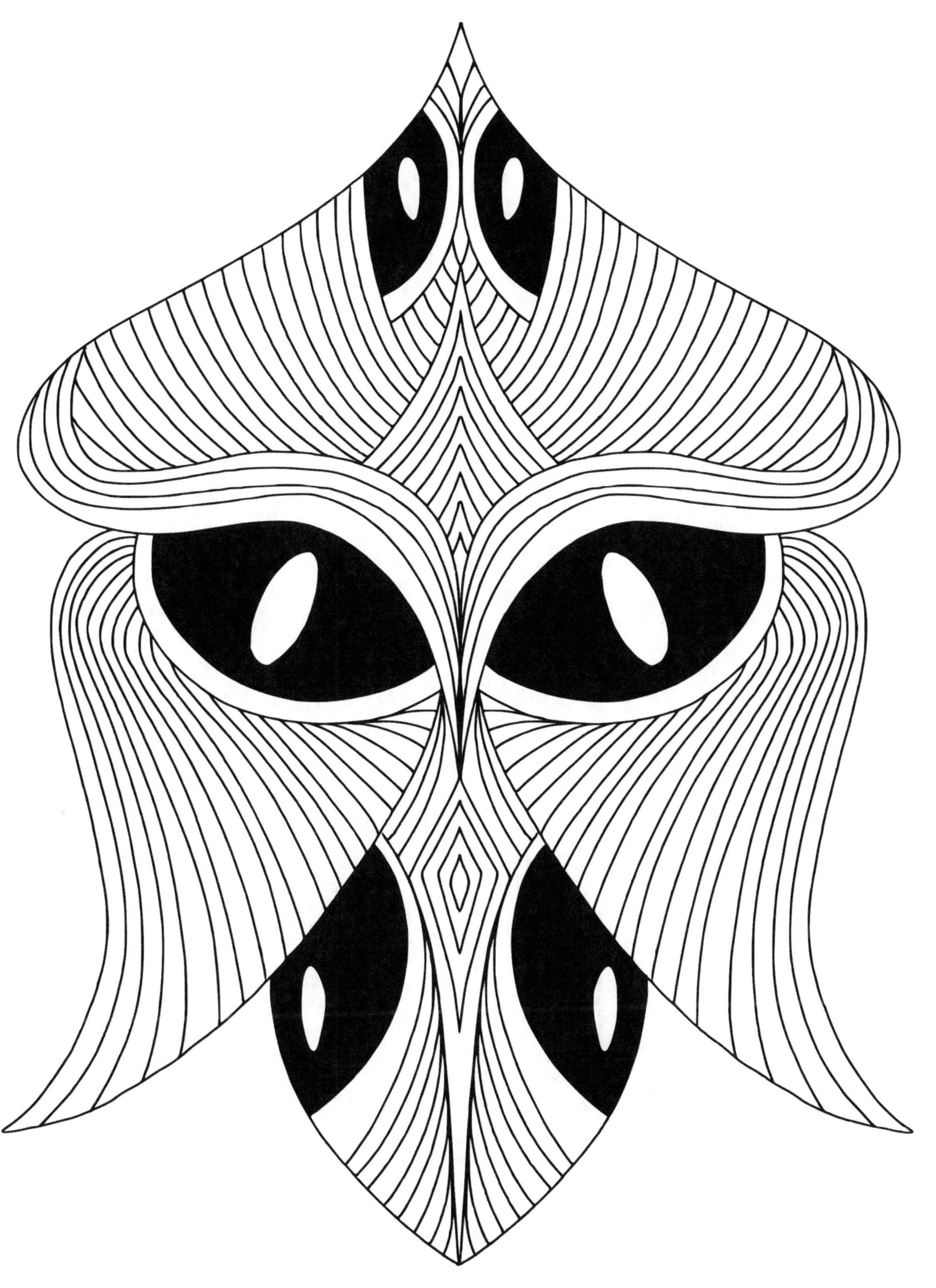

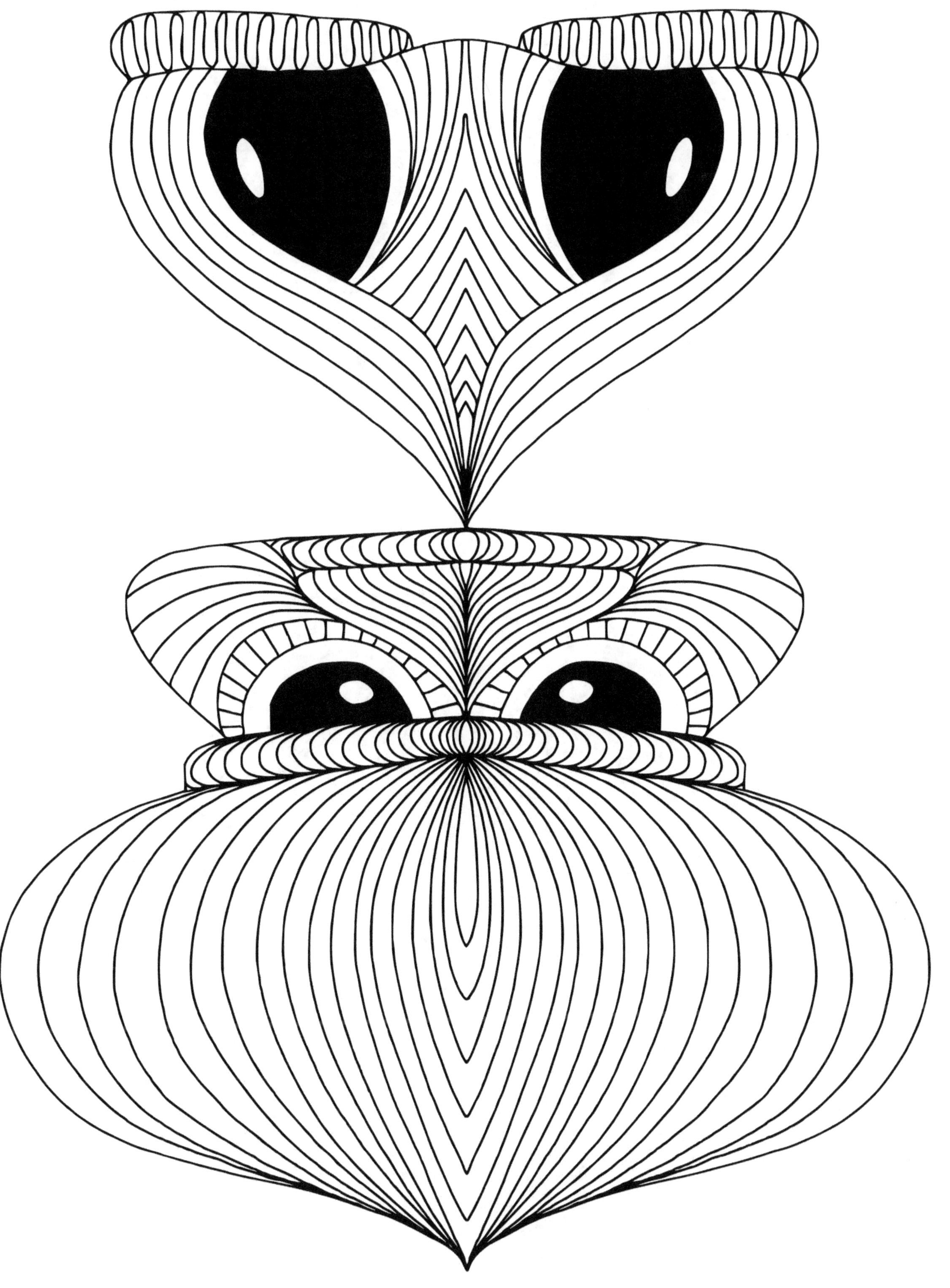

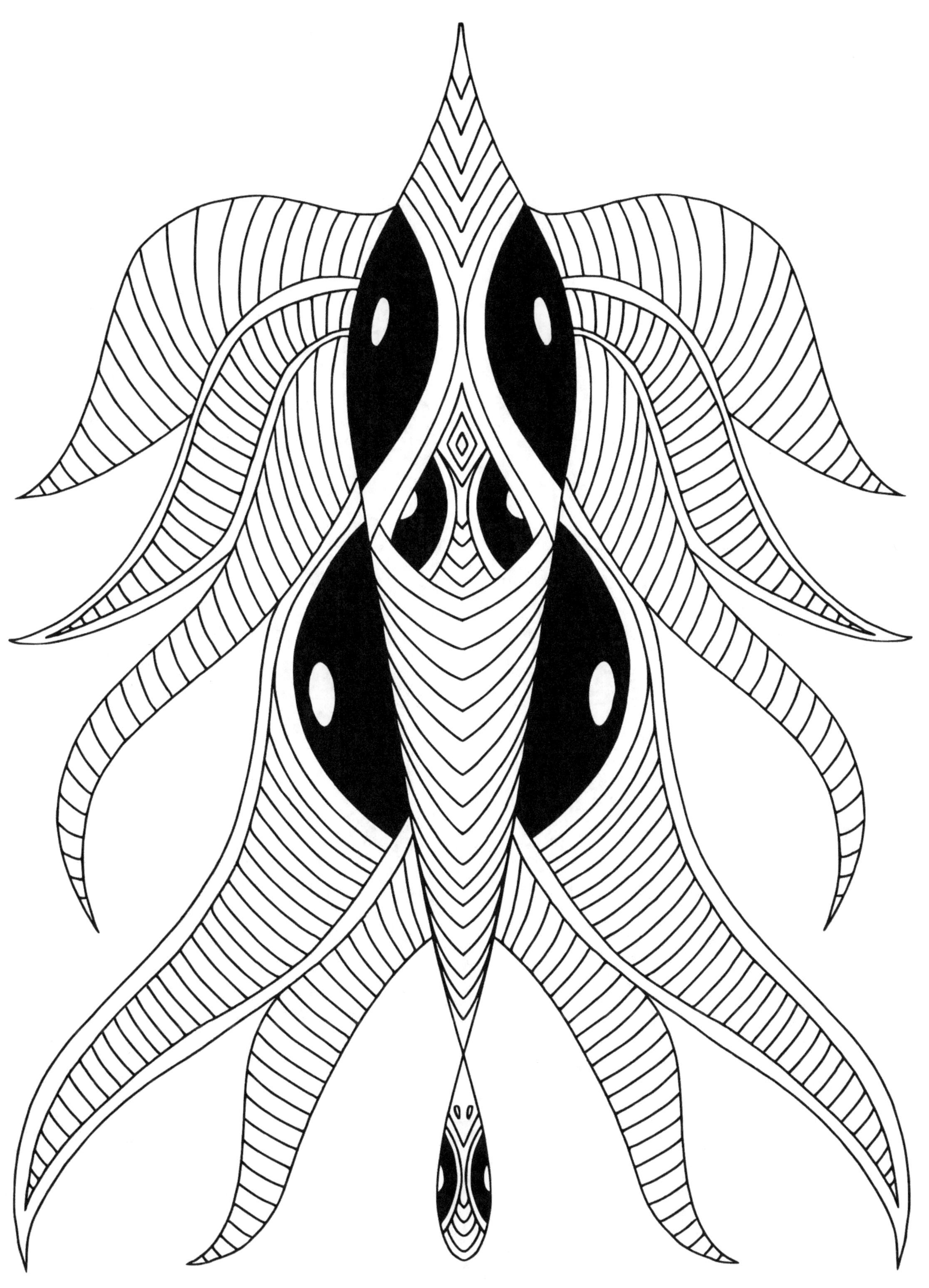

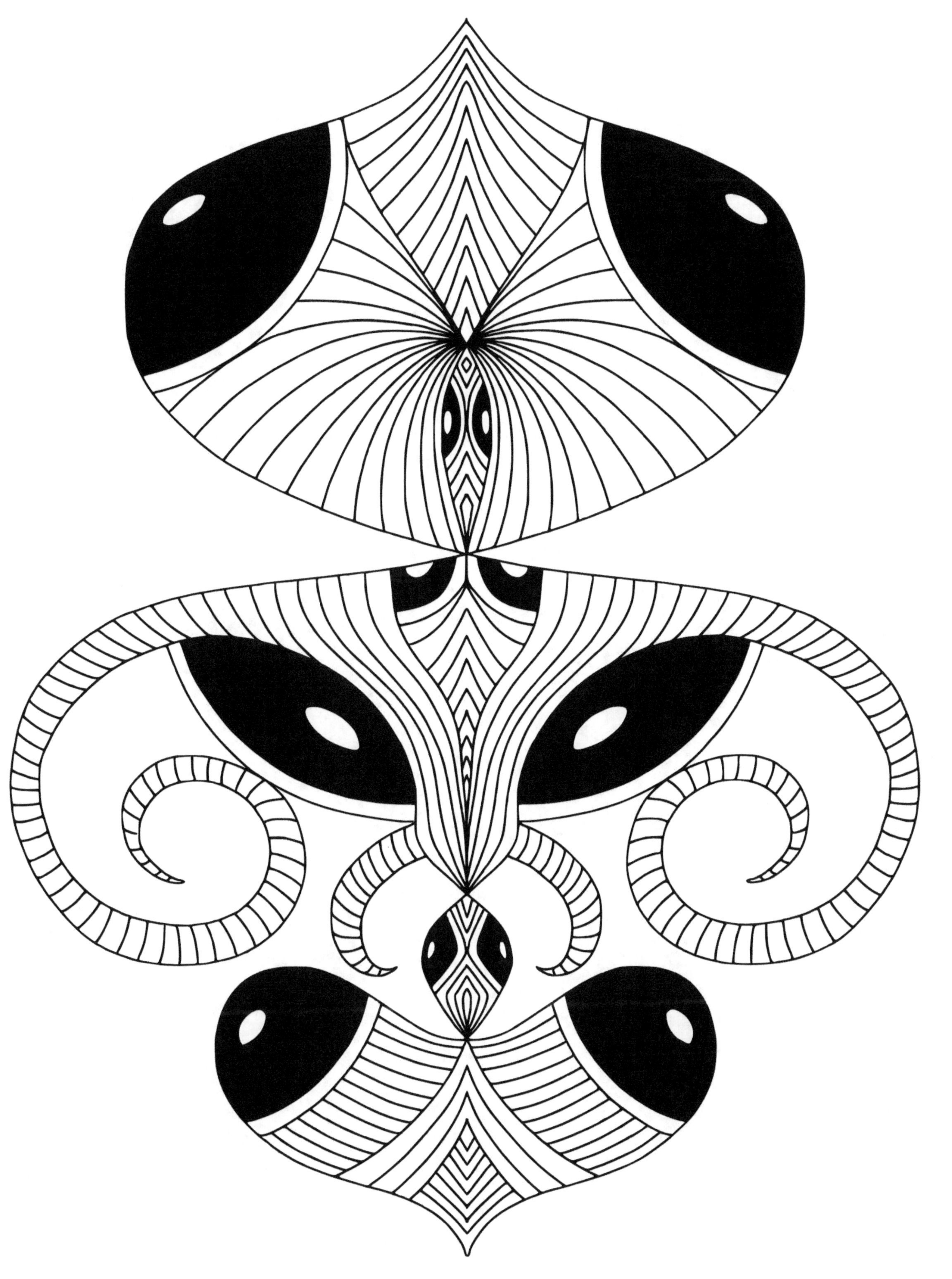

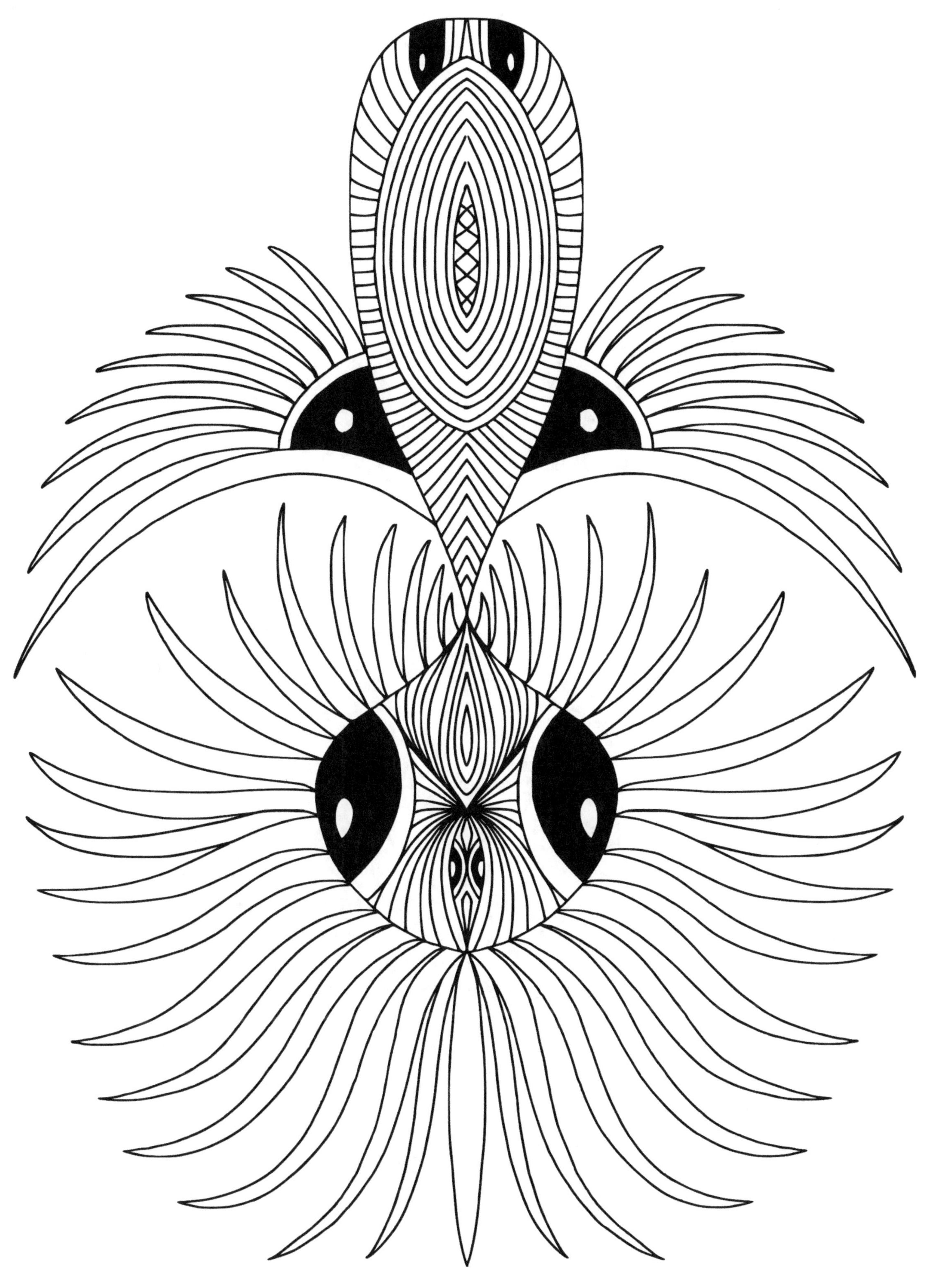

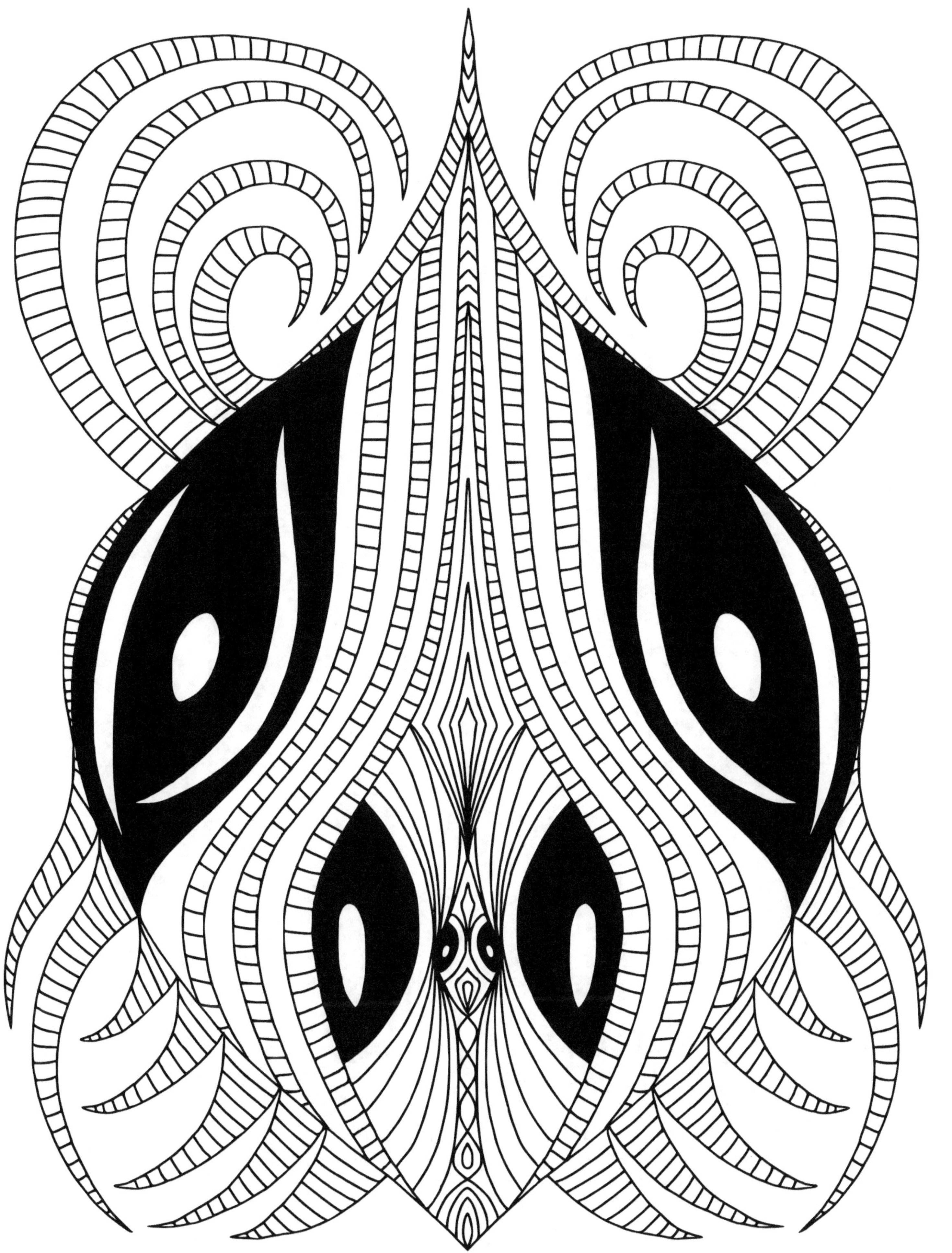

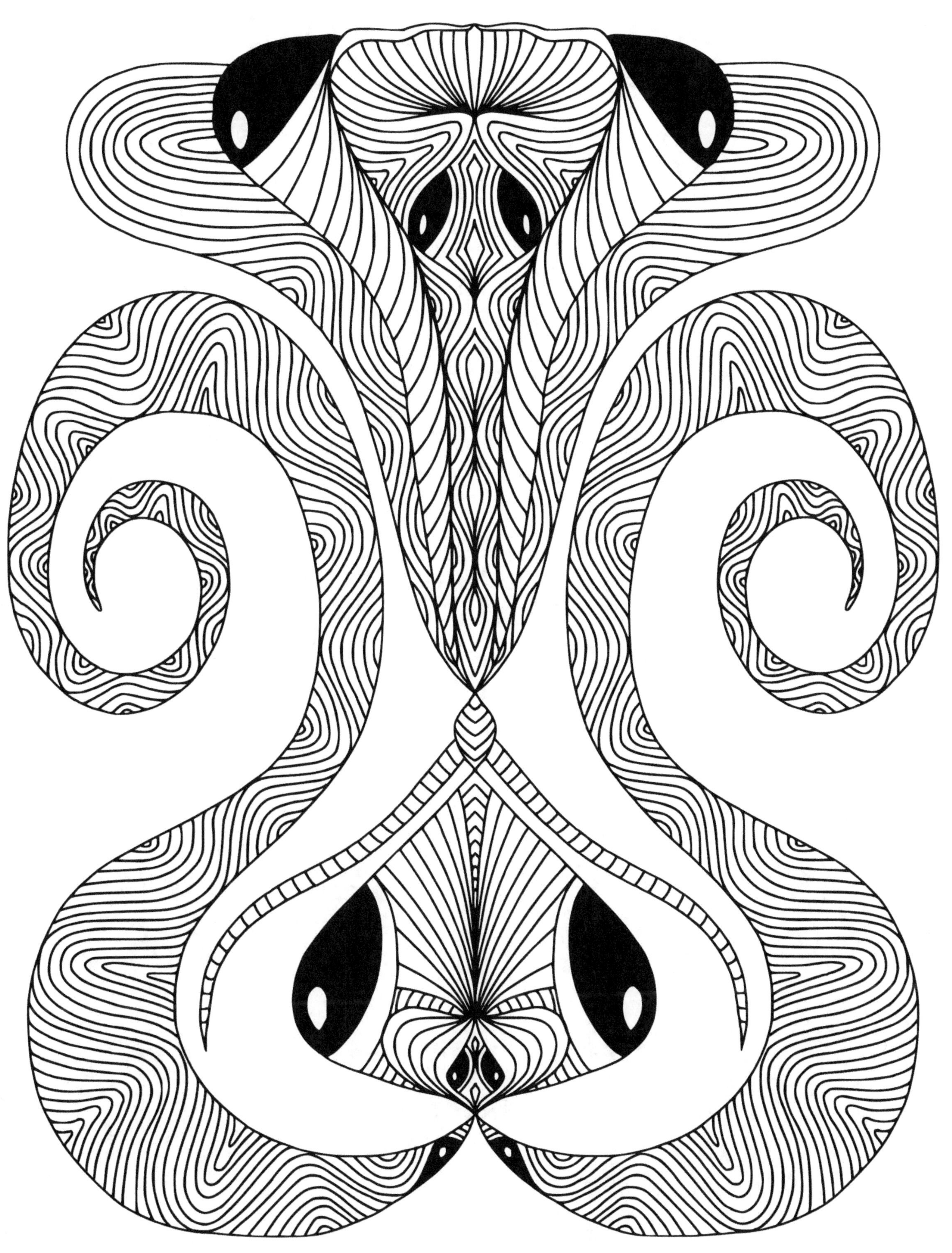

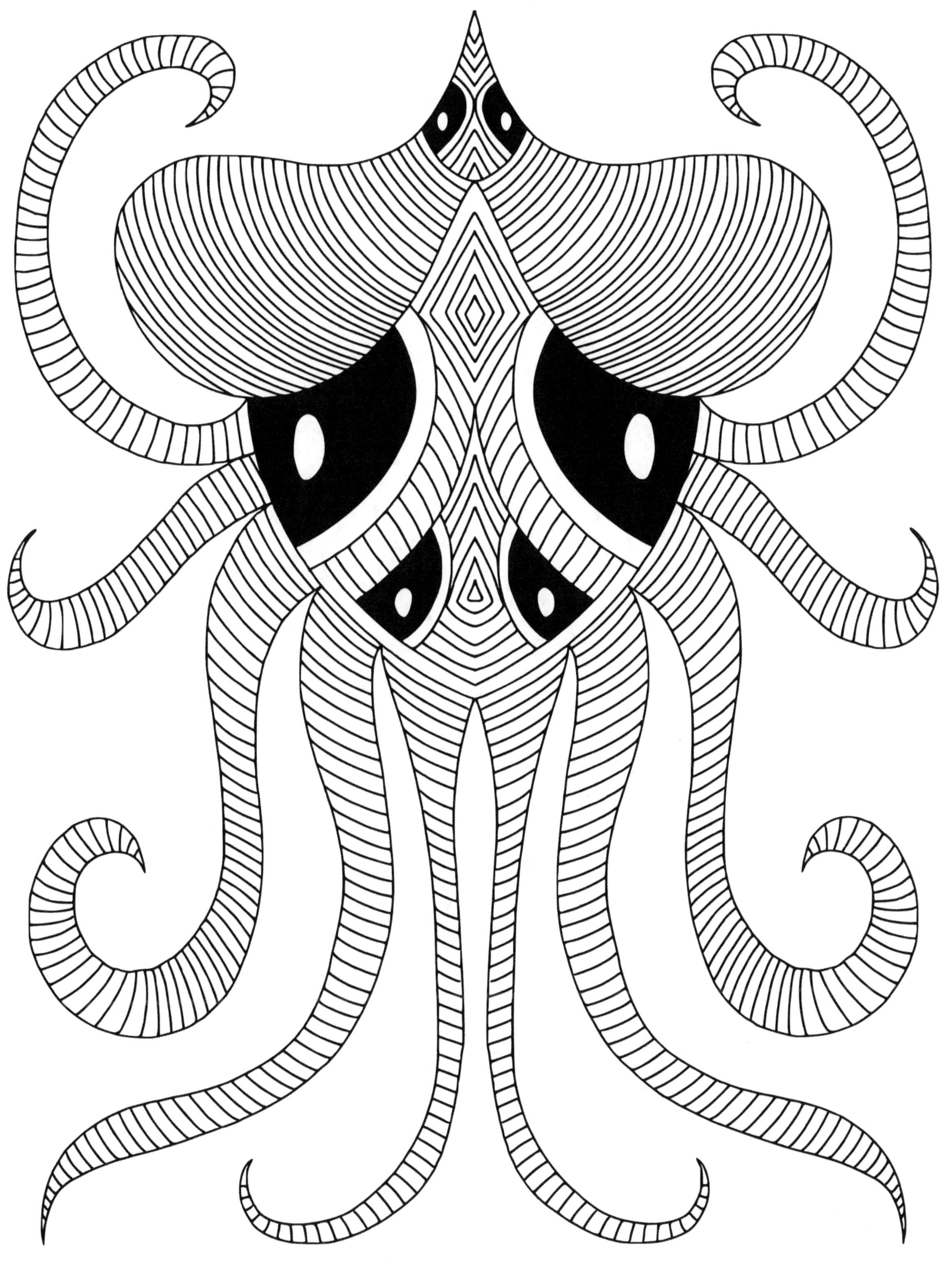

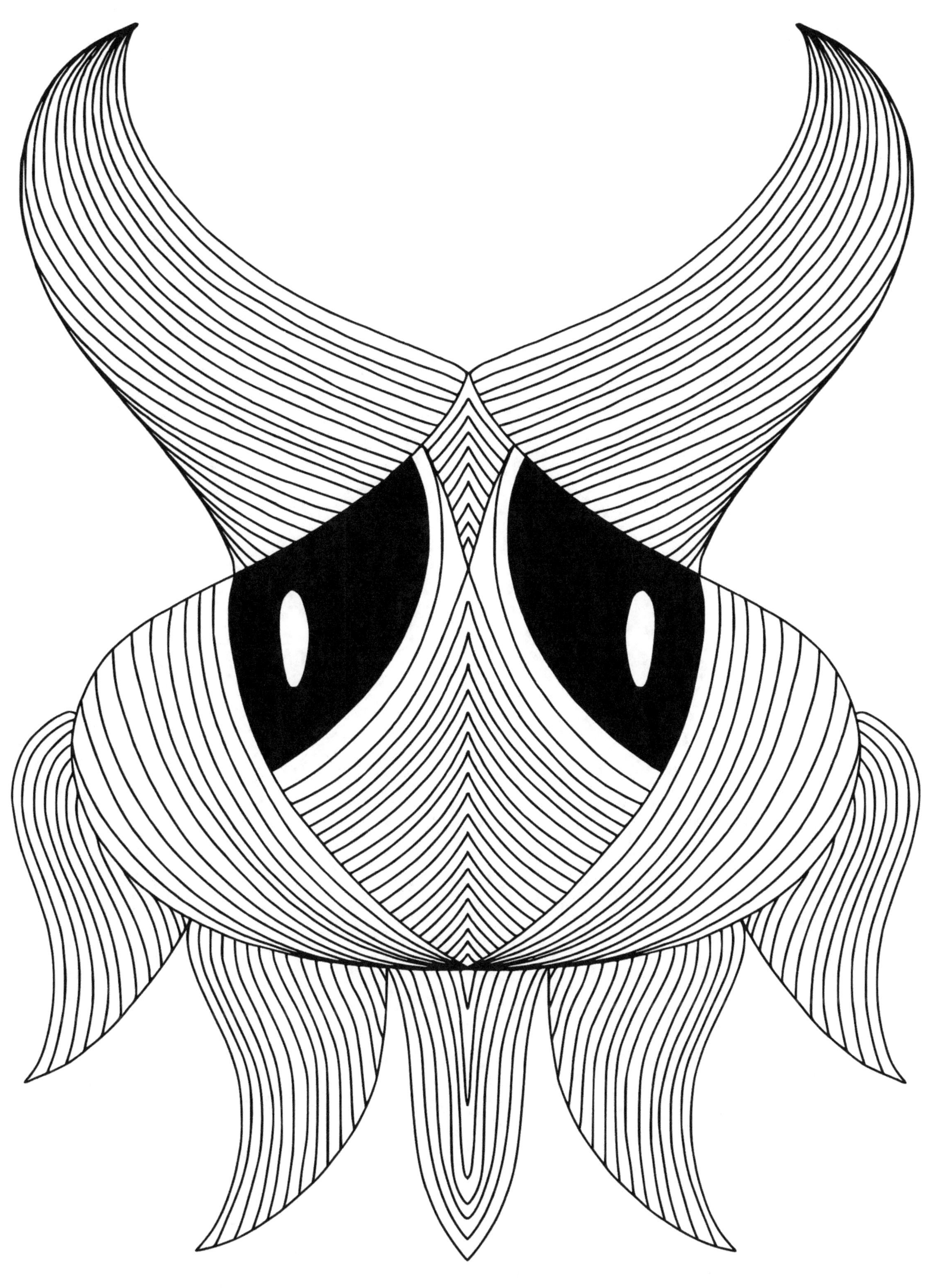

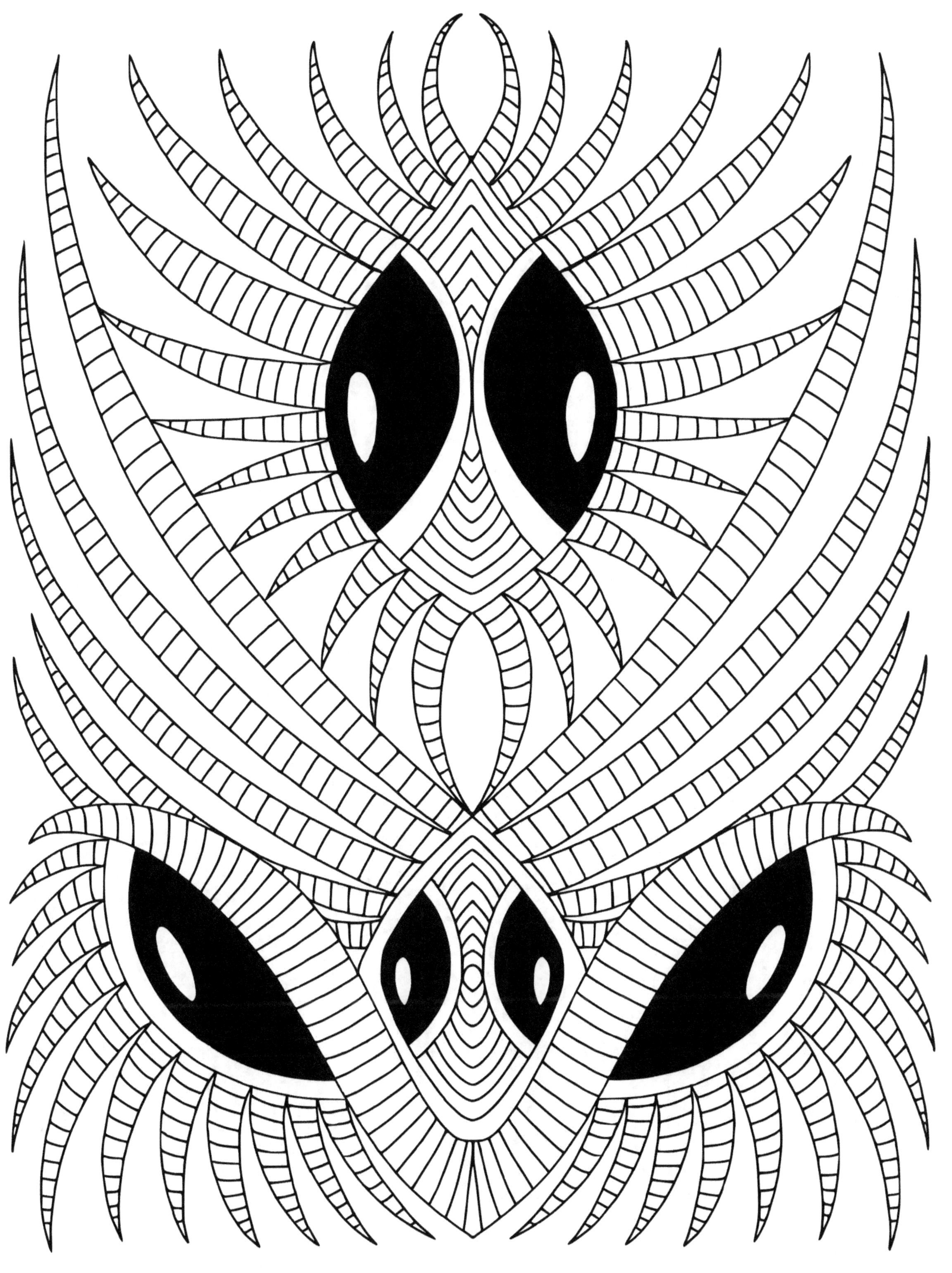

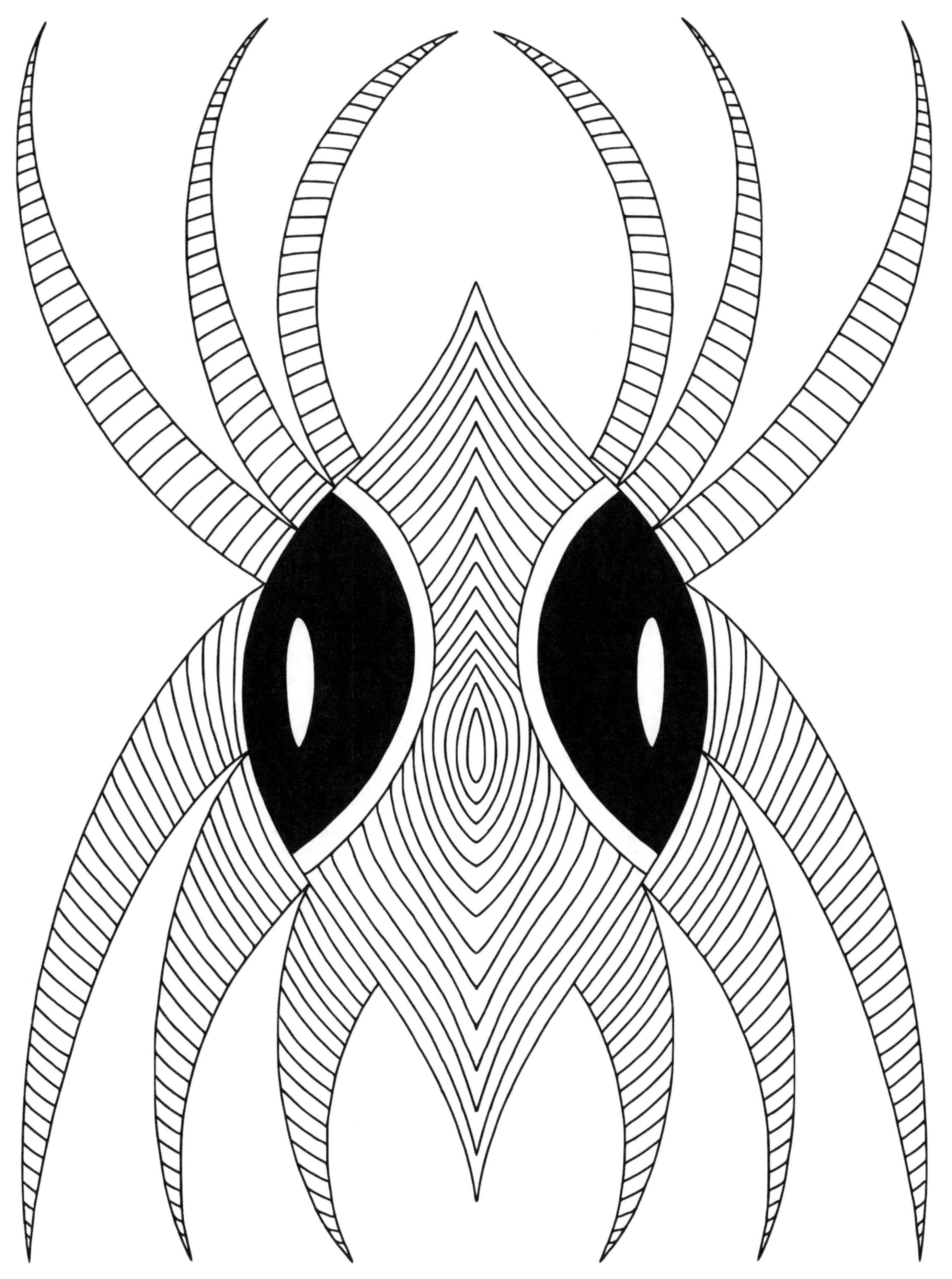

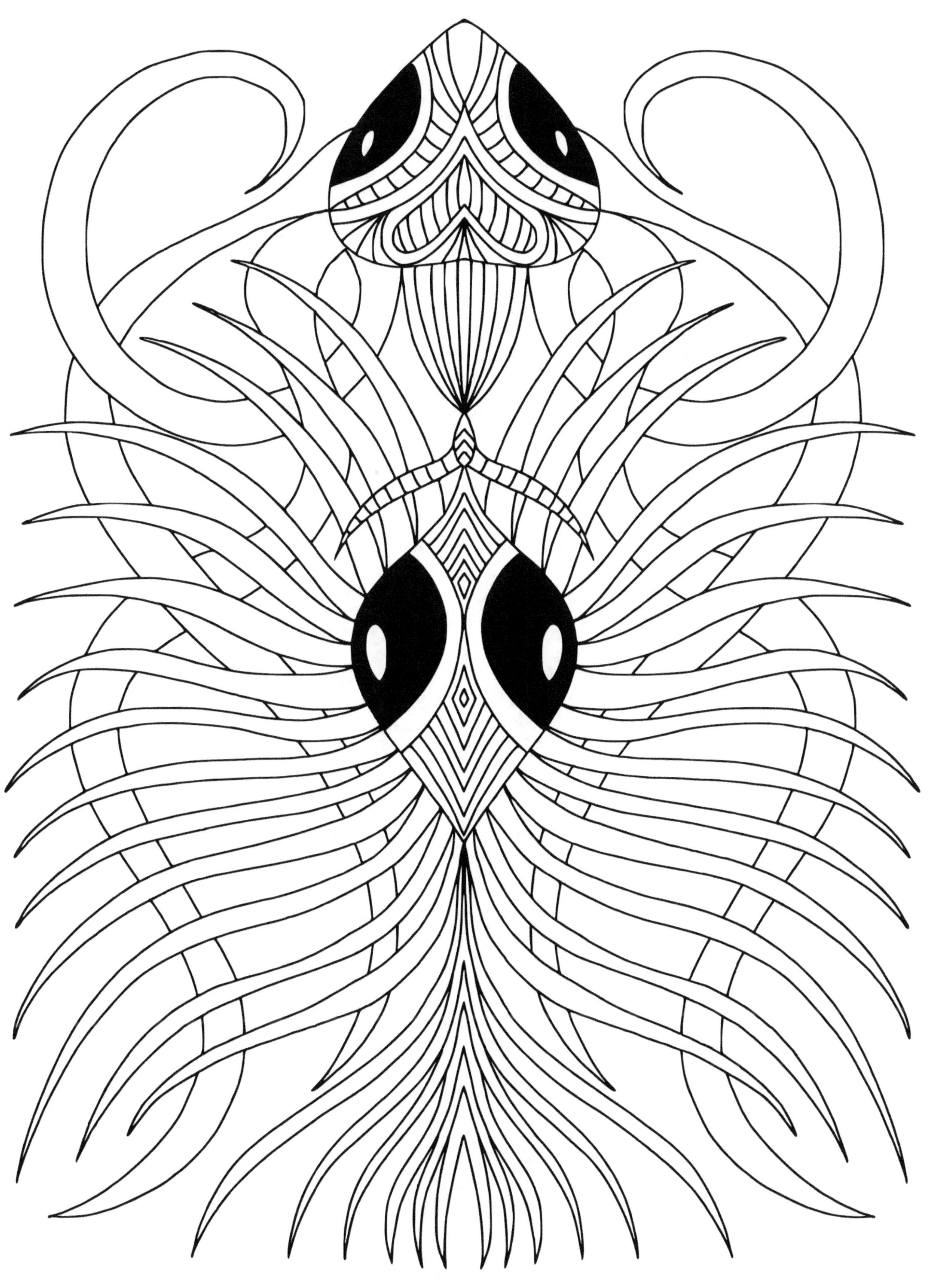

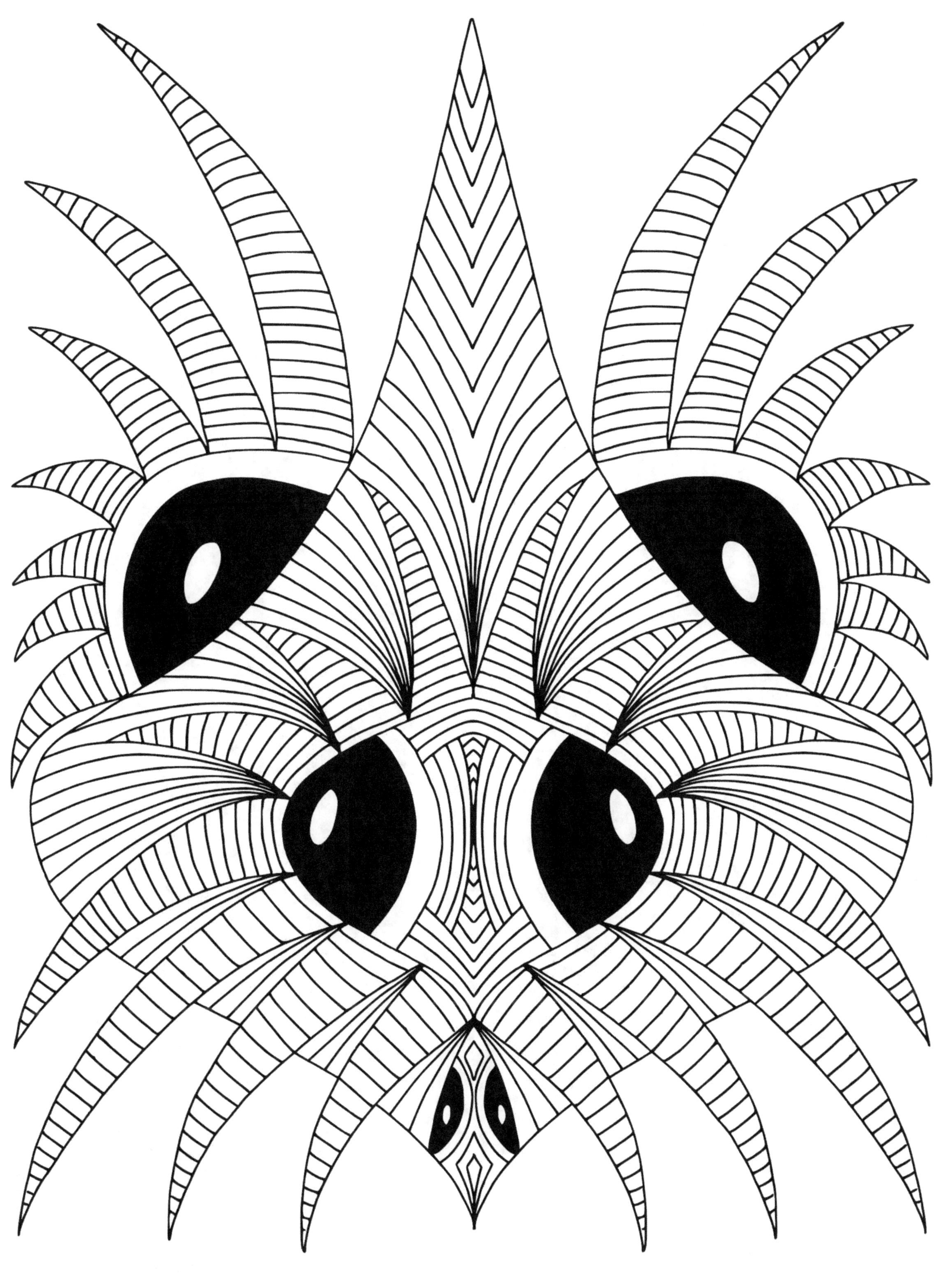

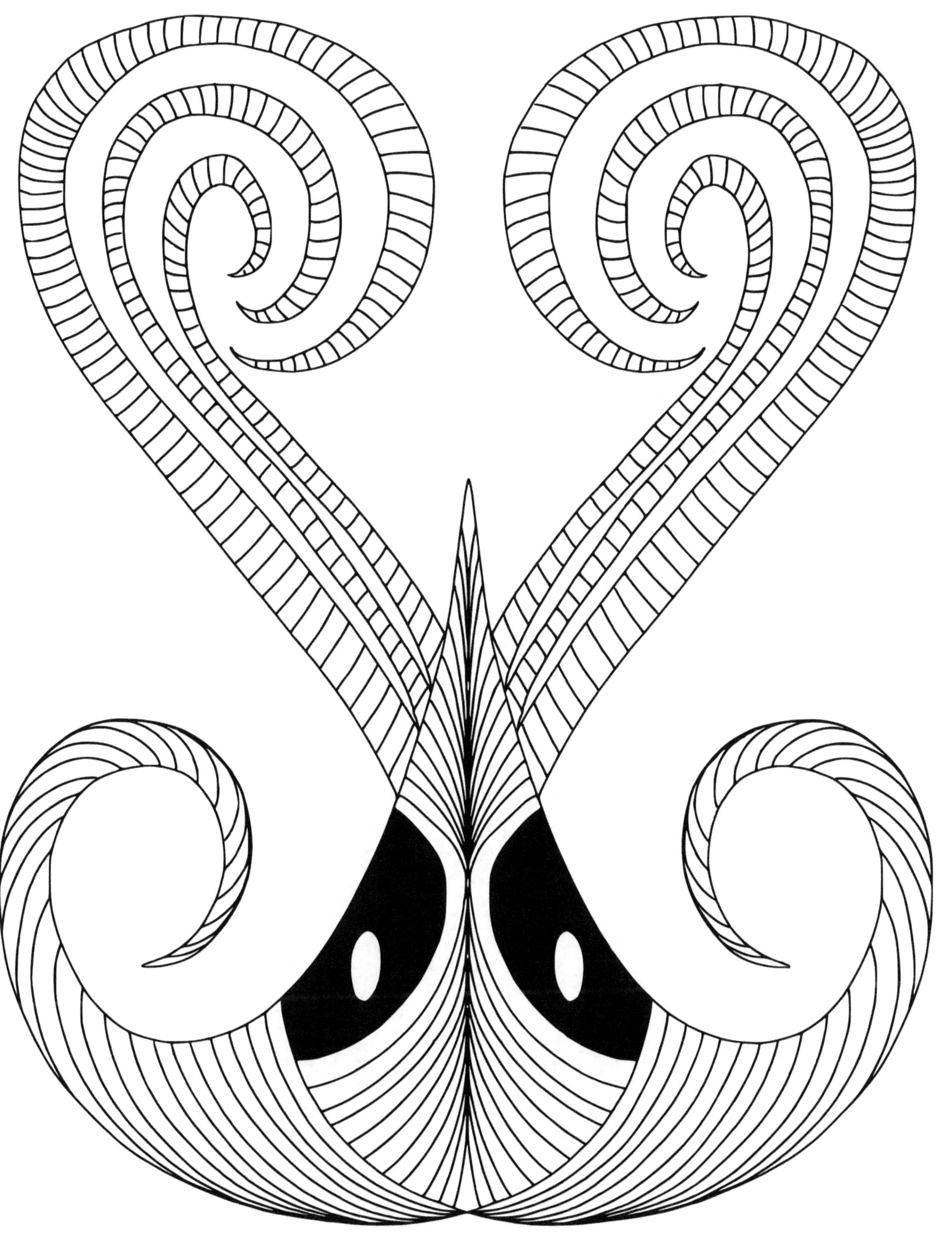

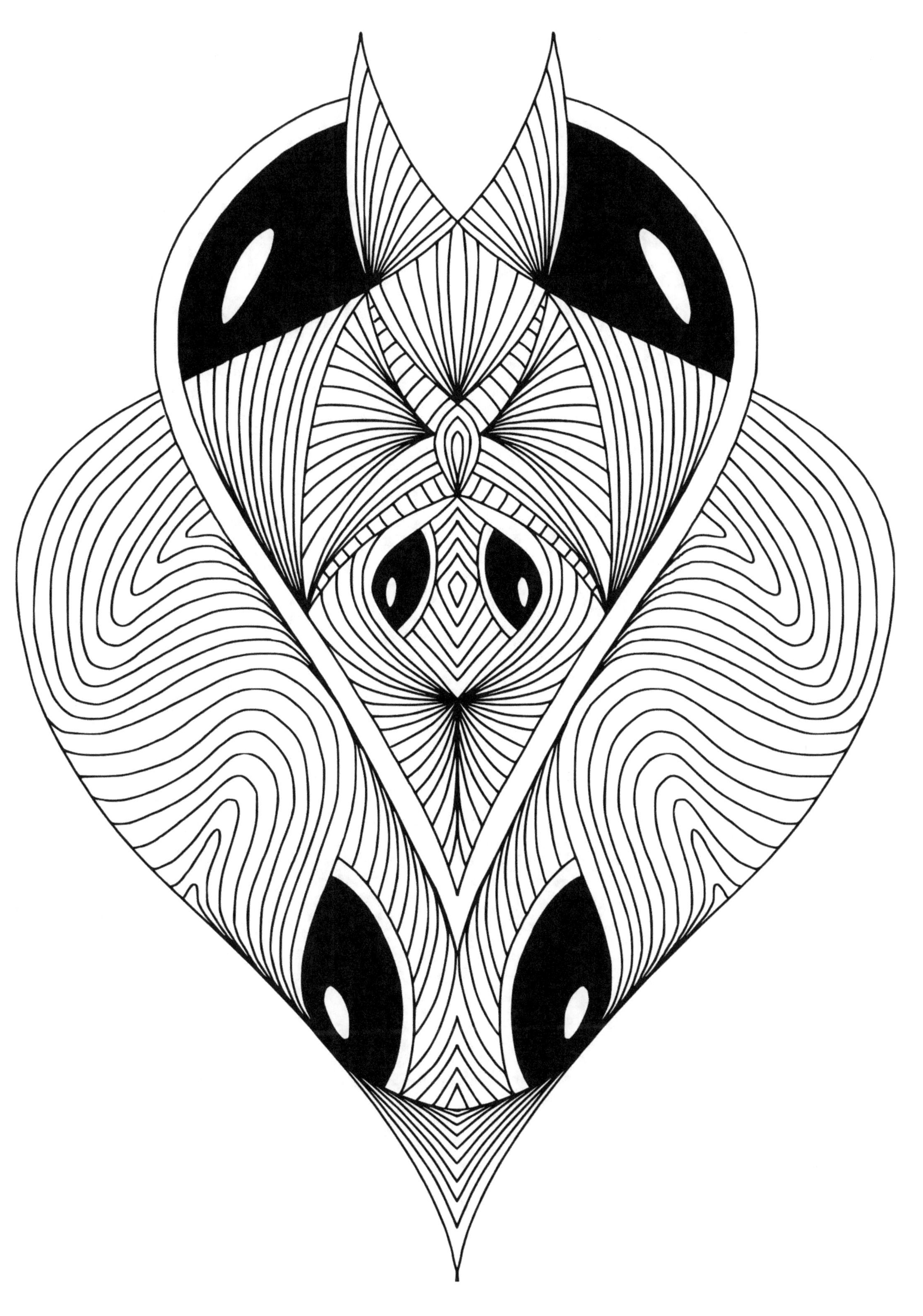

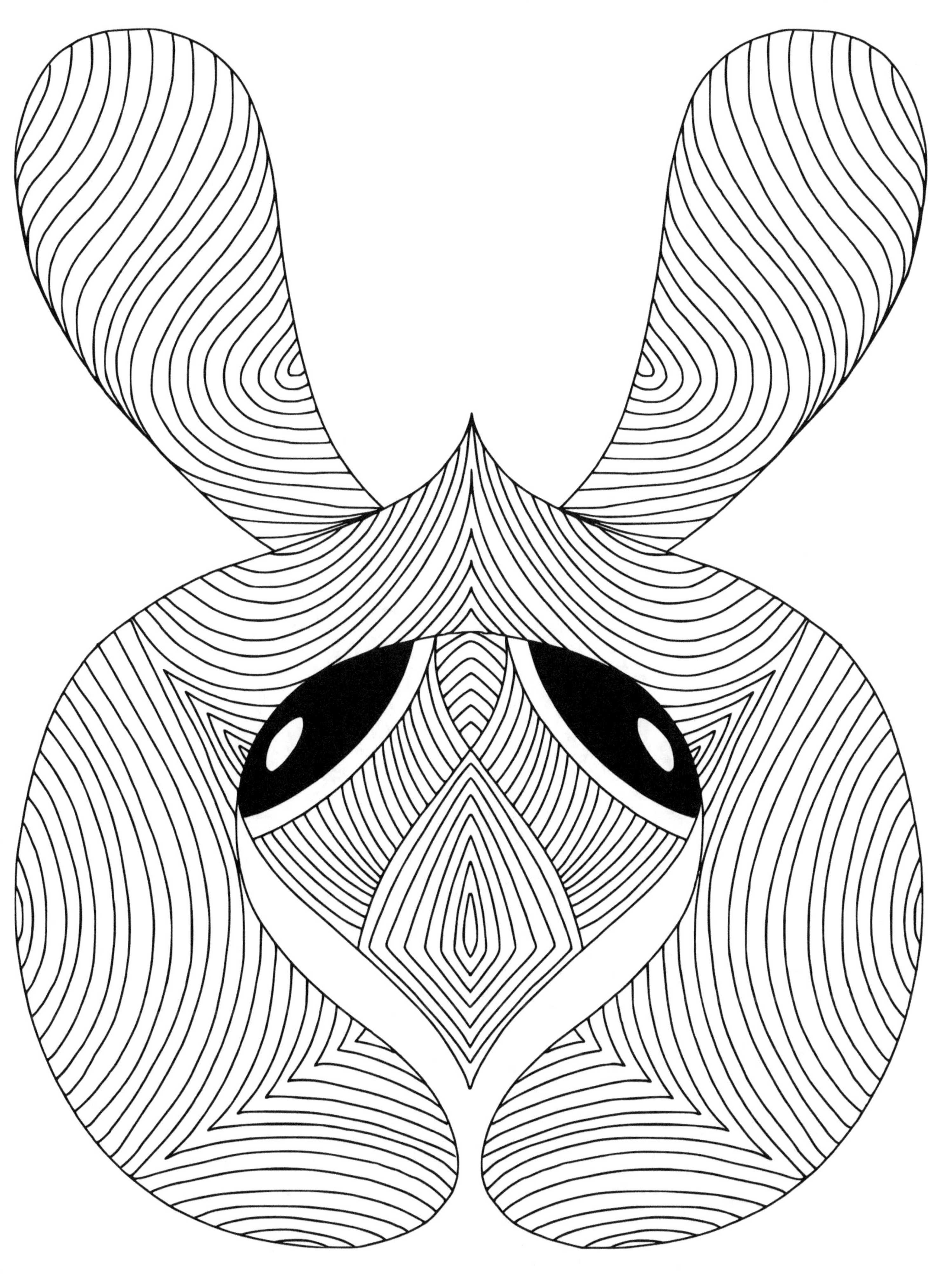

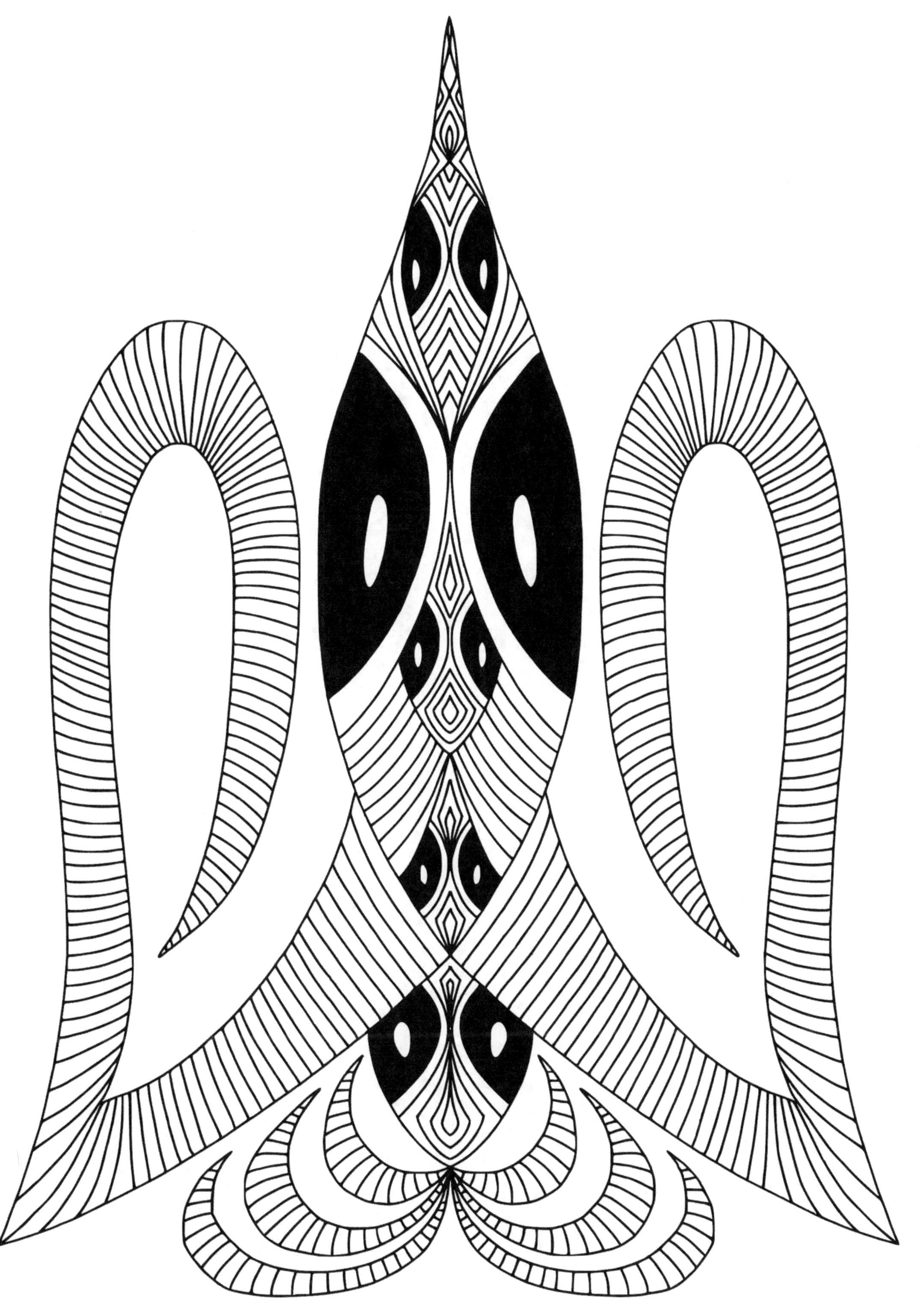

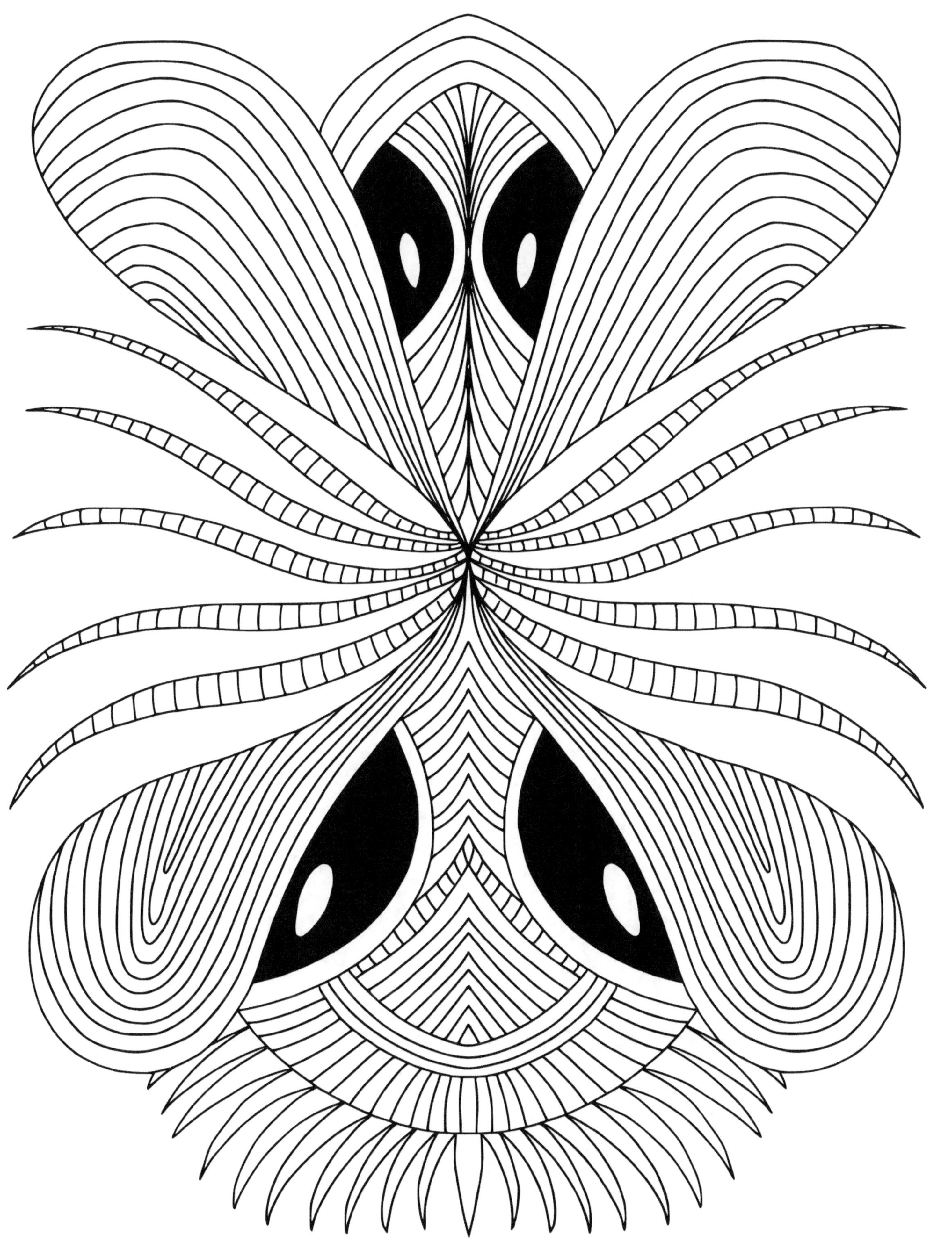

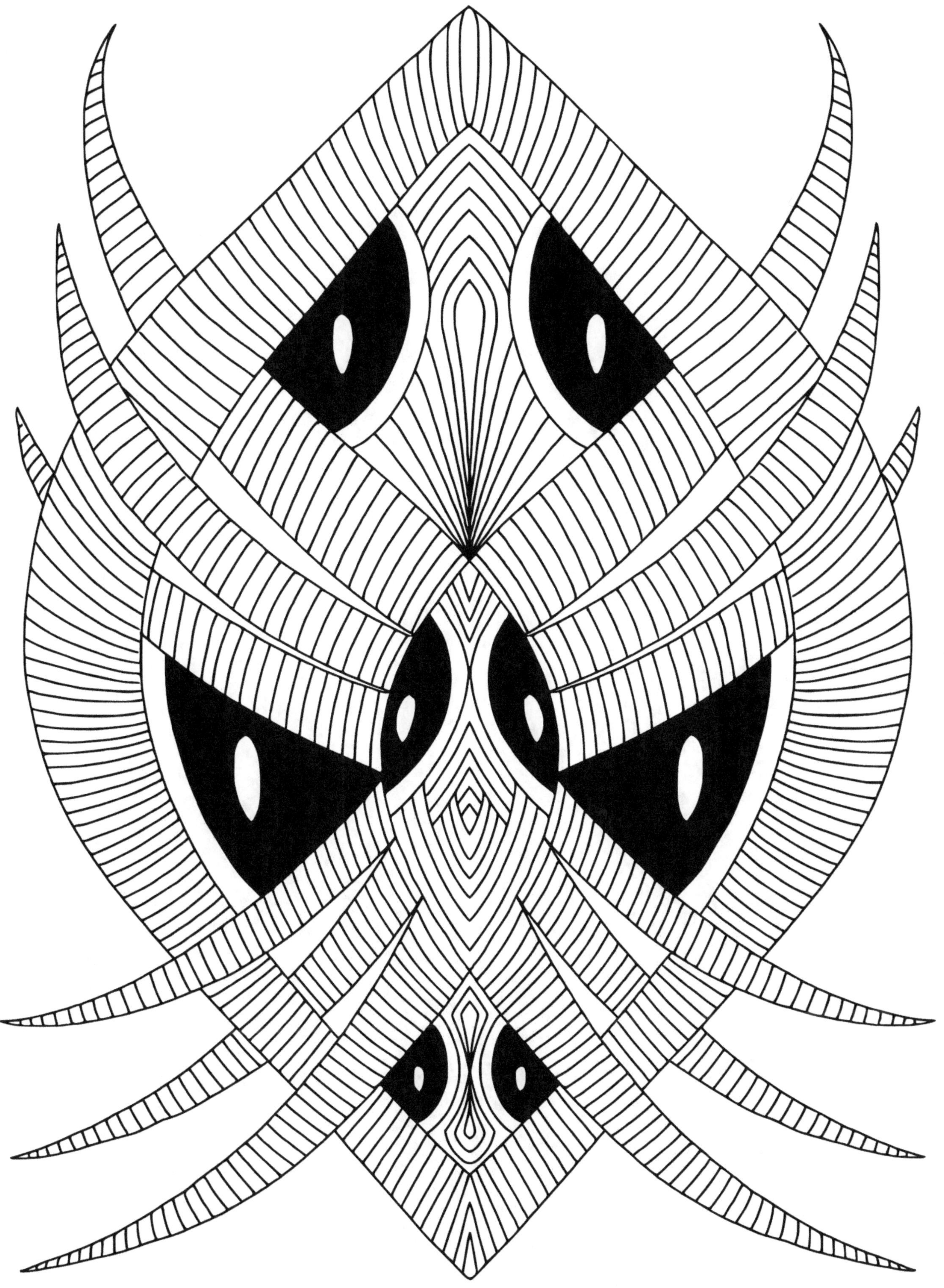

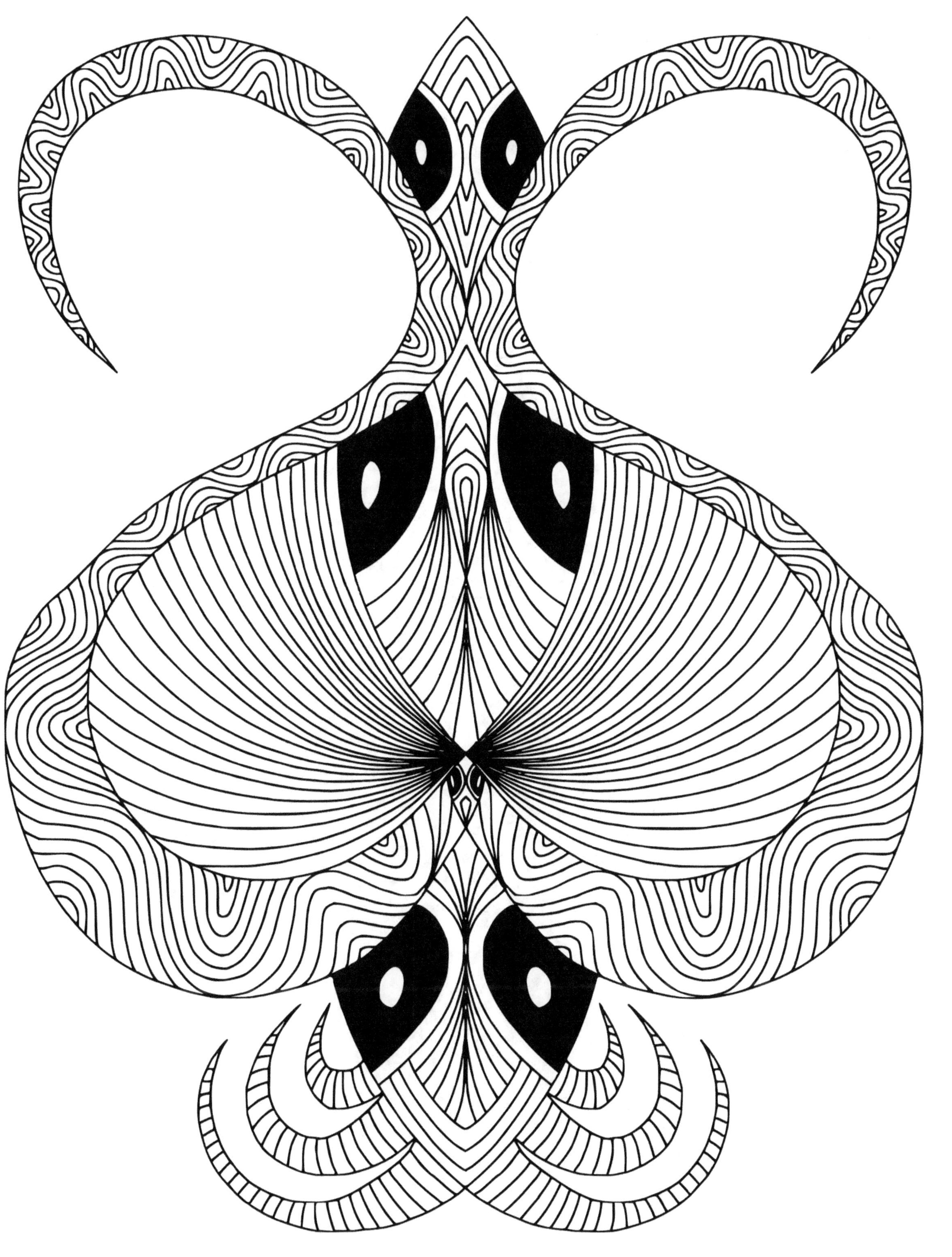

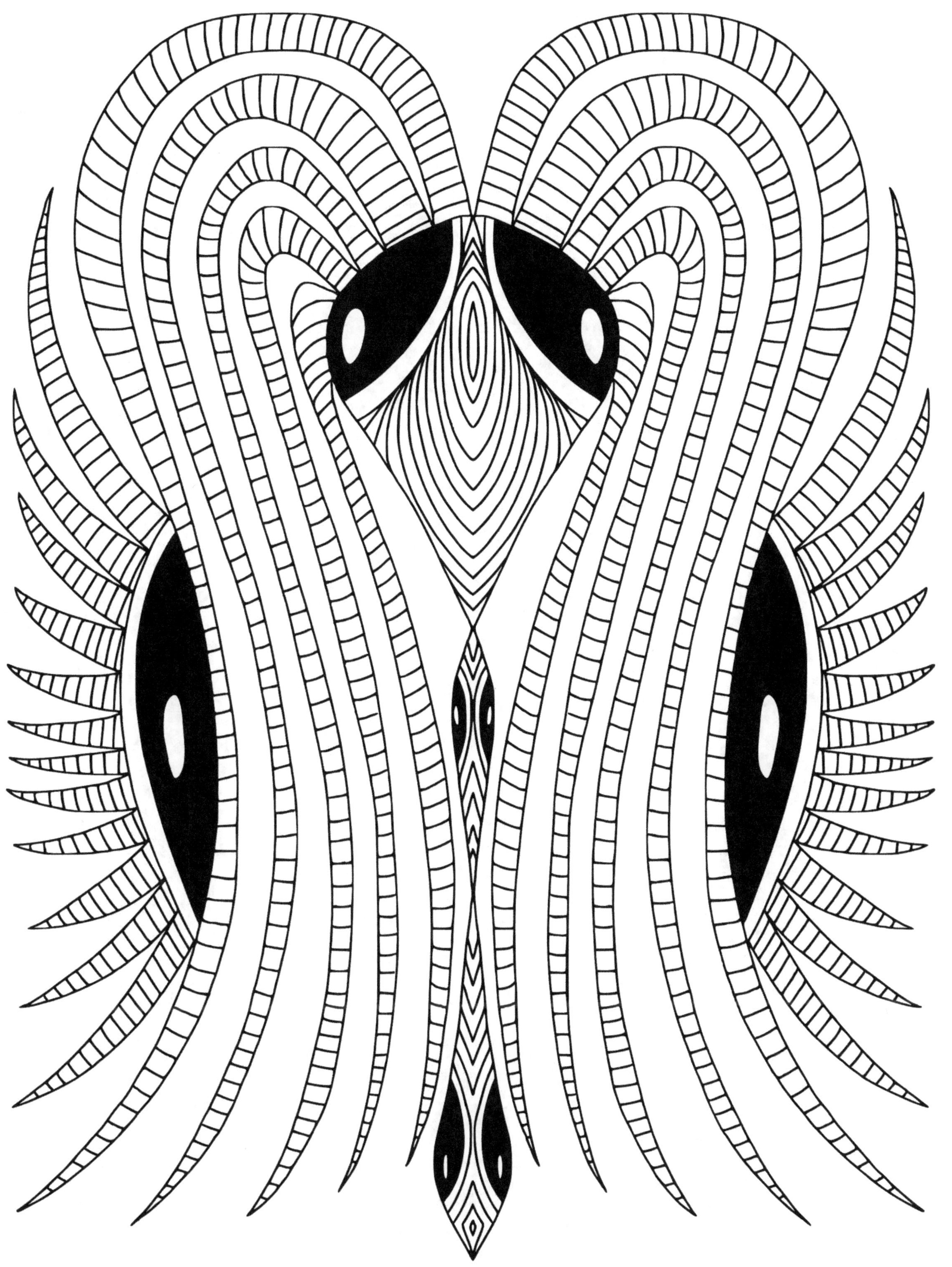

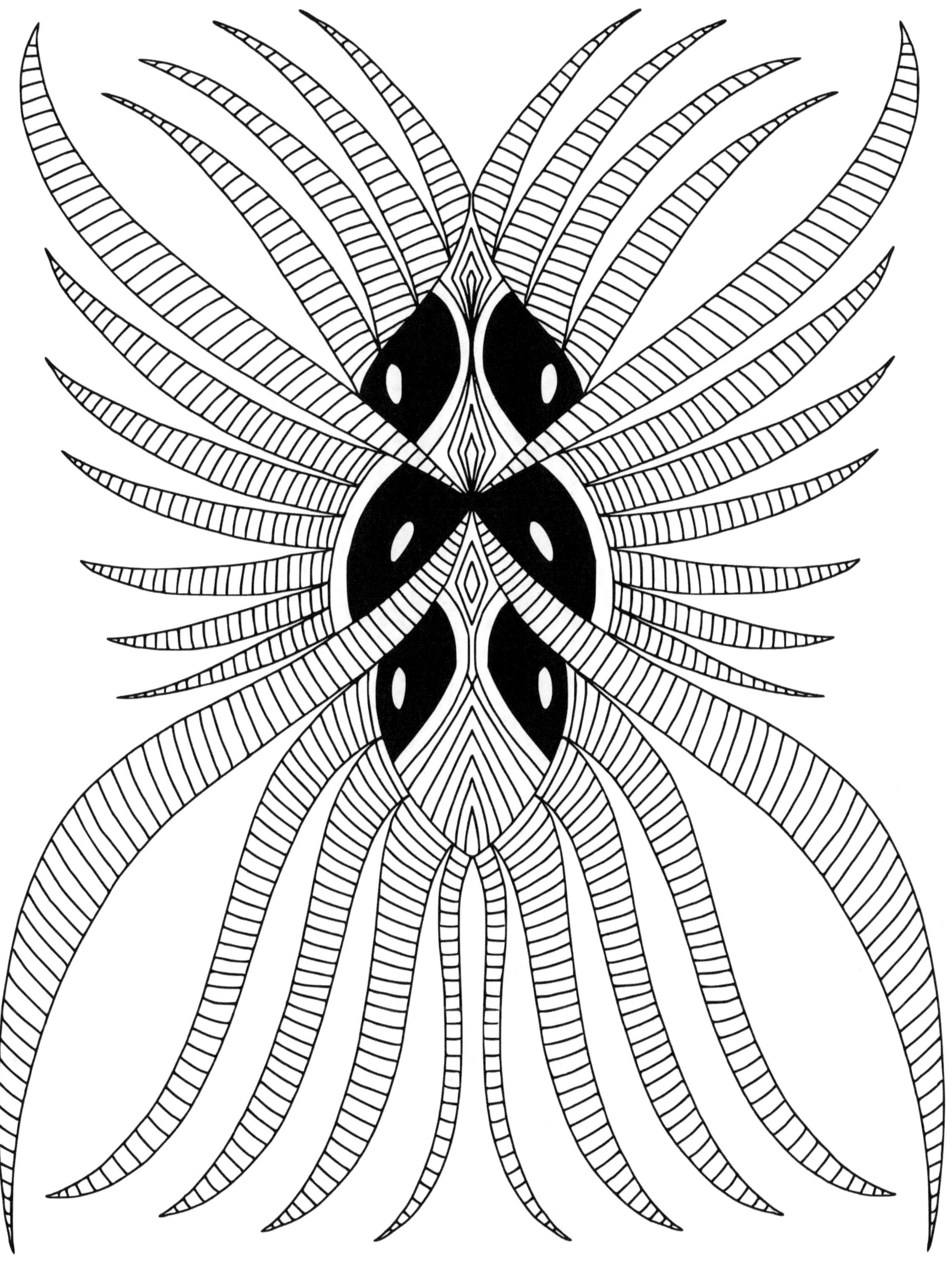

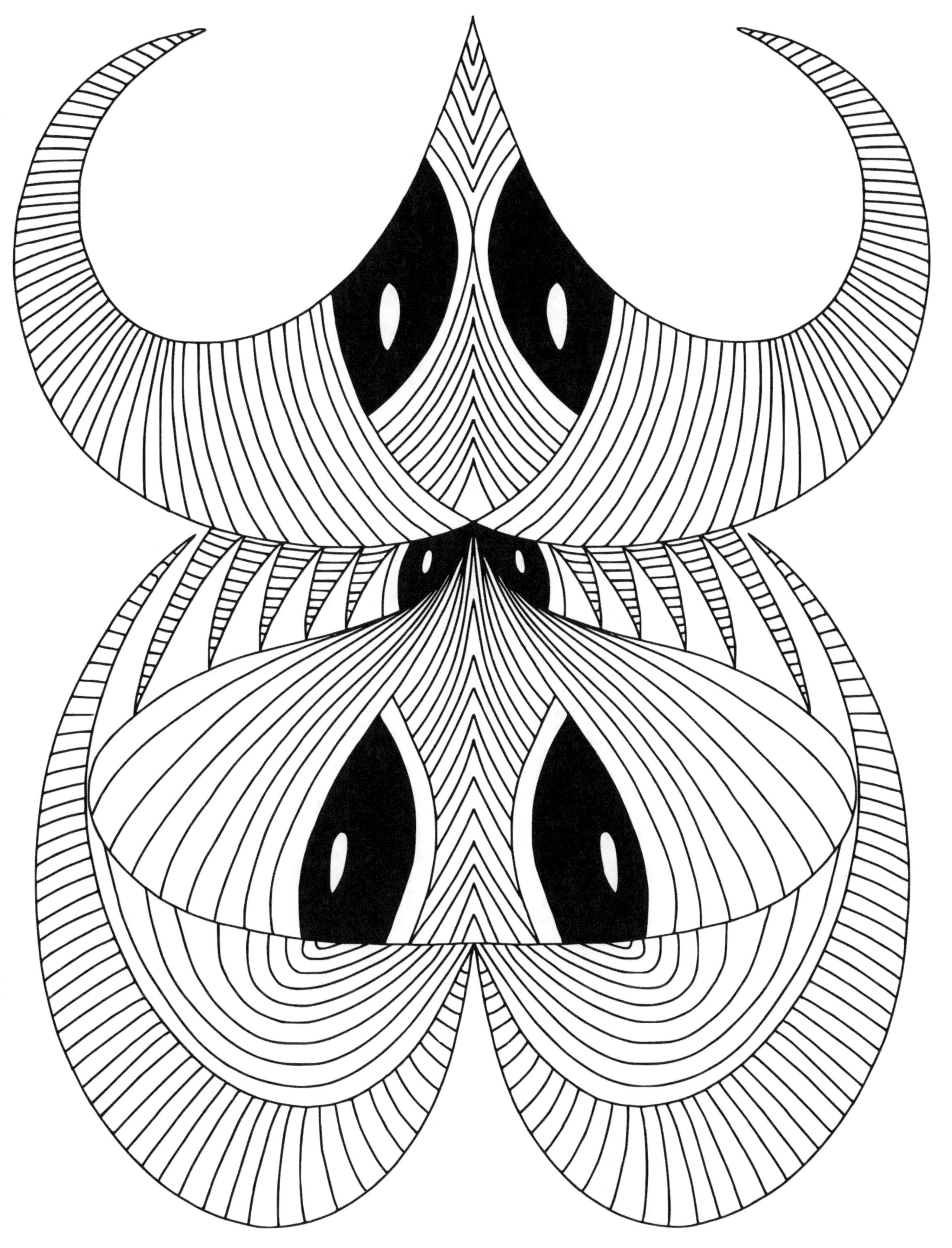

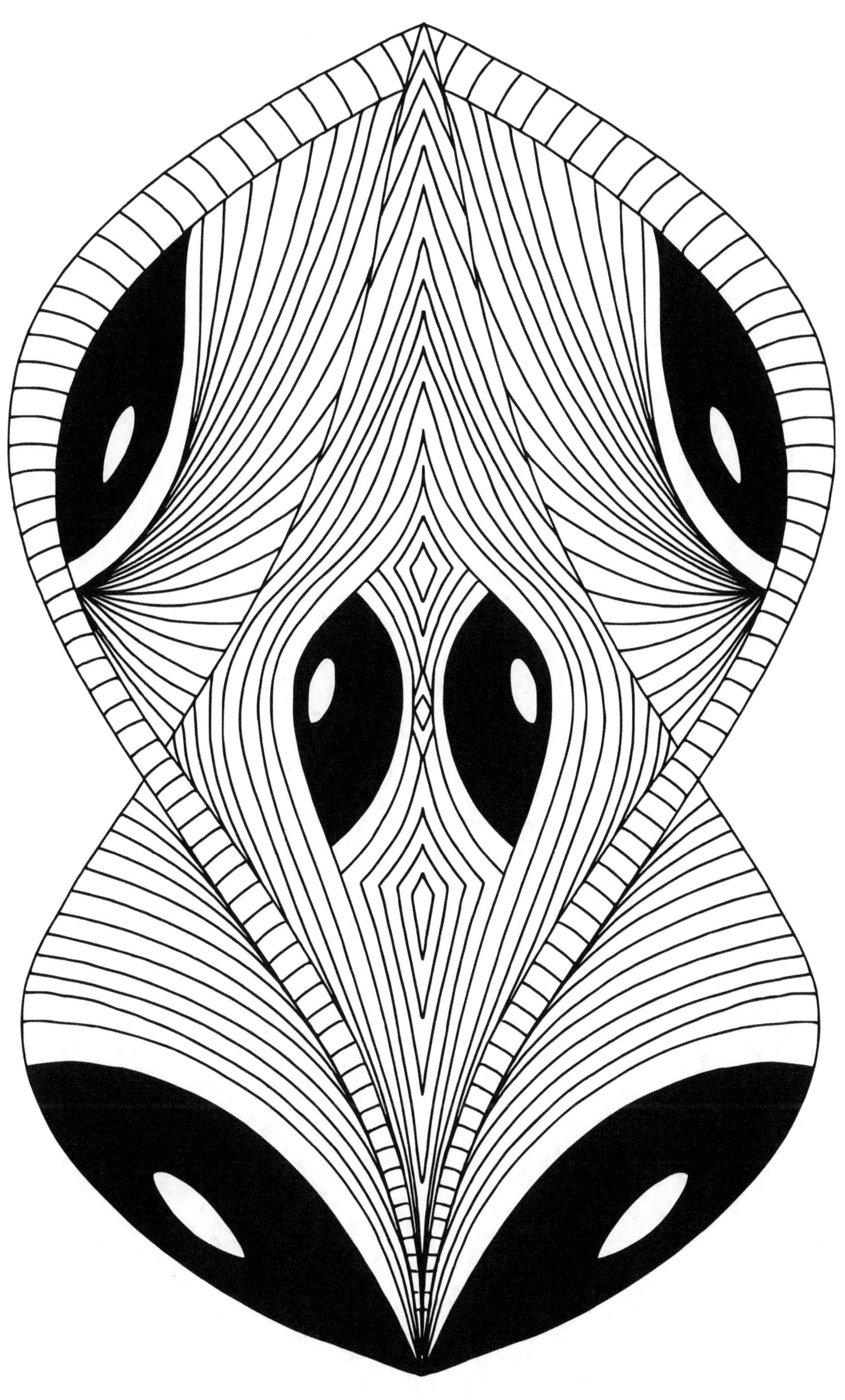

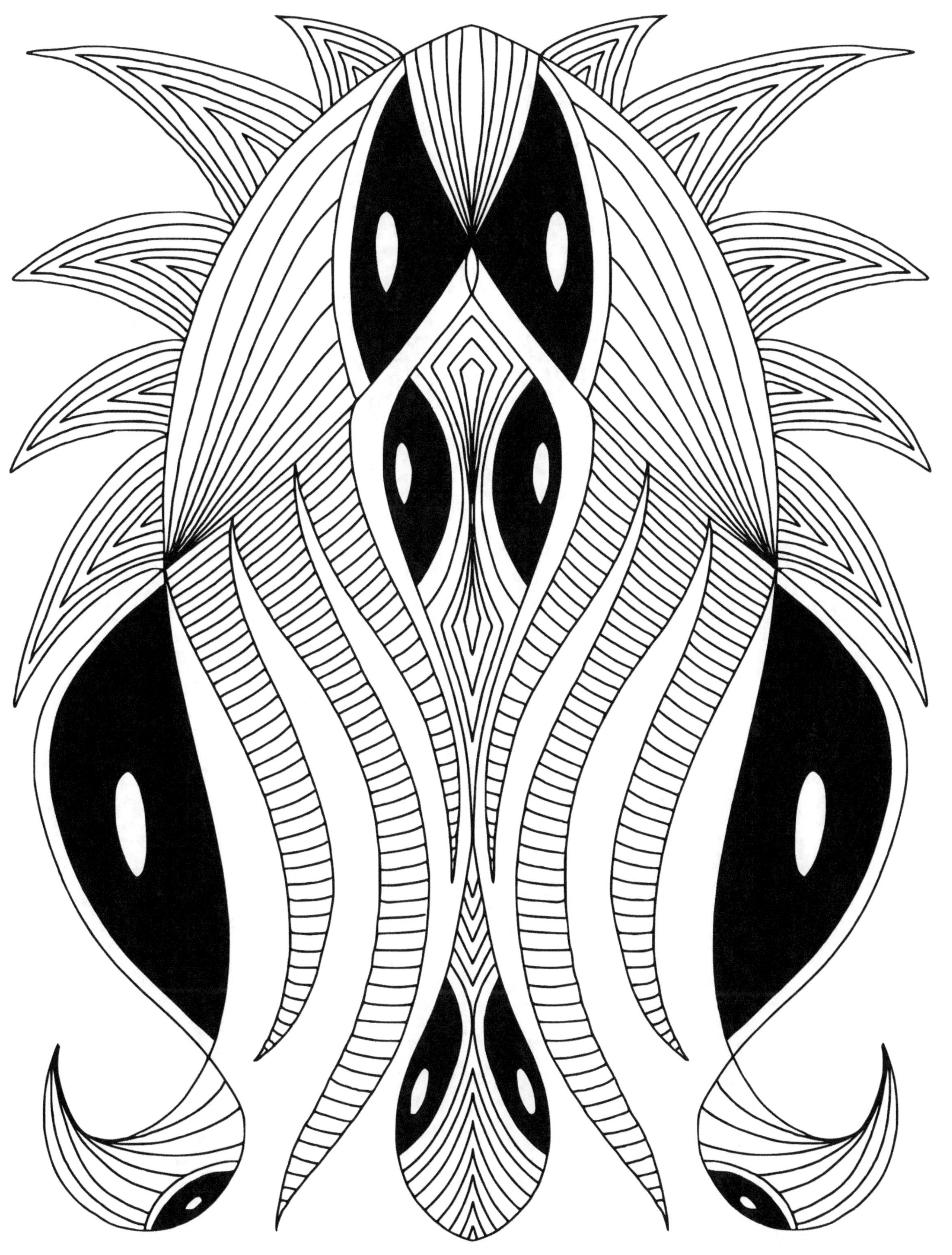

Test your colors here on the samples from
"My Pocket Coloring Companion"
&
"My Coloring Companion"

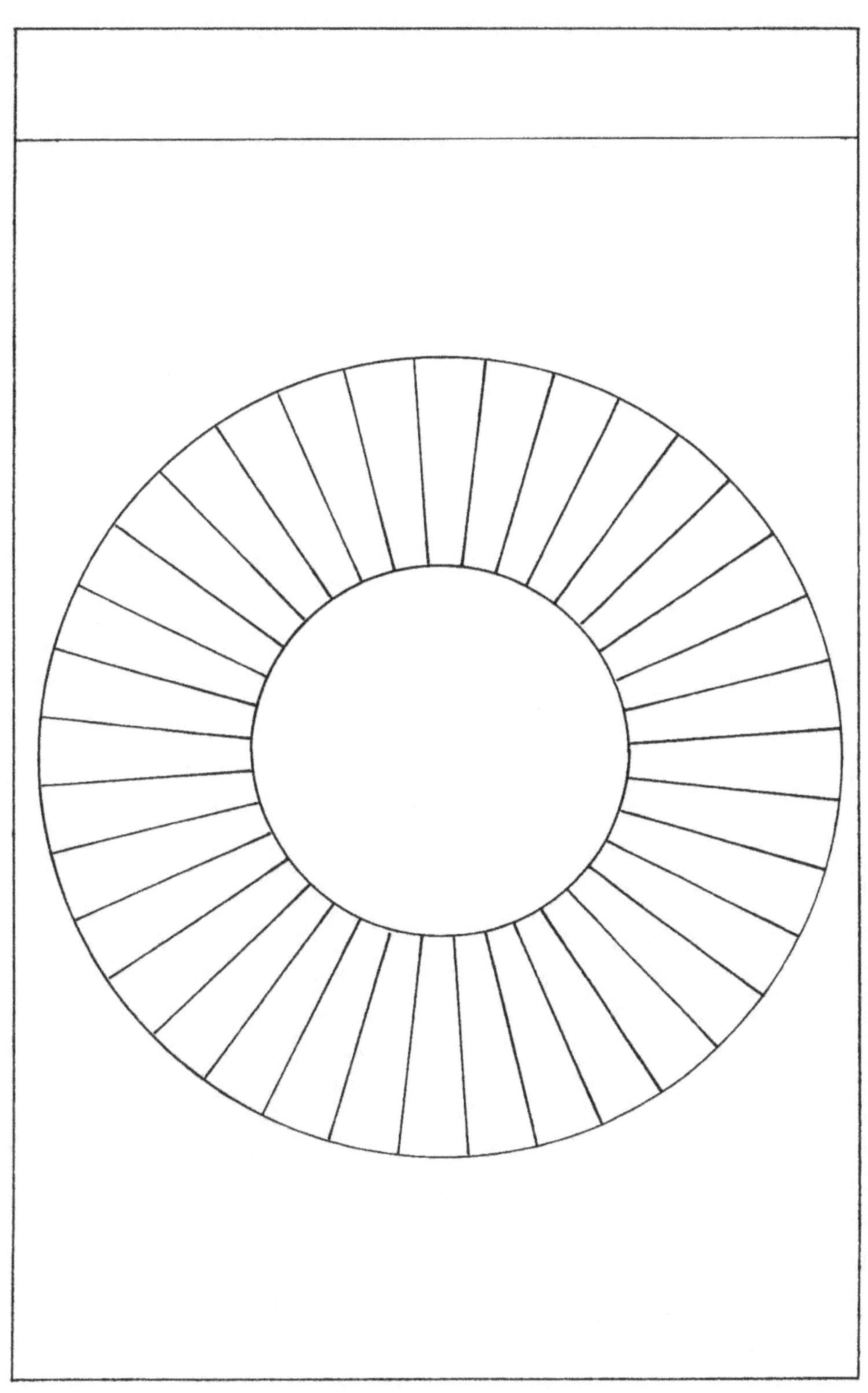

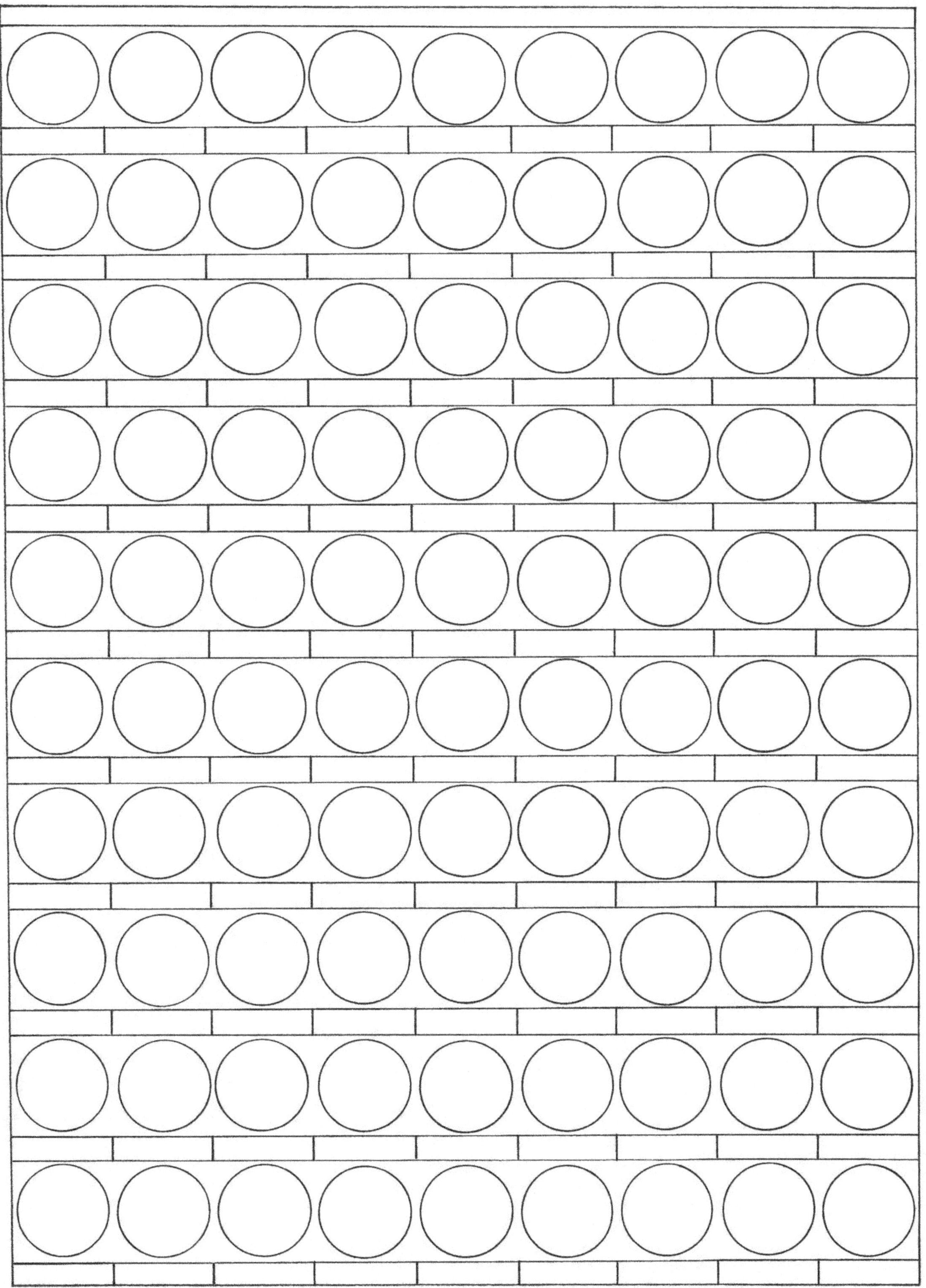